MAKING
SPACES
SAFER

D0979825

"Another world is possible but first we must talk about it and that's why Shawna Potter's book, *Making Spaces Safer* is so important. It helps break down big, scary concepts into ideas that are easy to understand and put into use. It doesn't lecture, instead it teaches and explains. It helps make this world a little safer for everyone."

—Lisa Snowden-McCray, Editor in Chief, *Baltimore Beat*

"By its very nature, punk is something that must always be shifting and mutating. The genre has made monumental changes over the last few years and as a result, the community around it is more inclusive and diverse than ever. But those changes have been hard fought. Shawna Potter has been one of the key figures on the front lines, leading the charge in where the punk scene is now and, more importantly, where it's headed."

—Dan Ozzi, writer at Noisey.com

"Punk made a promise of a freer, fairer, safer and saner world, but never fulfilled it. Shawna Potter has written a field manual for how, inch by inch and scene by scene, we get there. Now it's up to the rest of us to finally make it a reality."

—Spencer Ackerman, *The Daily Beast*

"As musicians and music fans, we've witnessed plenty of unsafe situations that venues couldn't or wouldn't resolve—not because they didn't care, but because they just didn't know how to do better. *Making Spaces Safer* has so many clear tactics for making shows more inclusive and welcoming, and, as a side effect, more fun for everyone. Whether you book bands, tend bar, want to look out for the wellbeing of your fellow music fans, or own the whole damn club, this book has great tips that will help you make your space rule."

—Sadie Dupuis, of Speedy Ortiz

MAKING SPACES SAFER

A GUIDE TO GIVING HARASSMENT THE BOOT WHEREVER YOU WORK, PLAY, AND GATHER

Shawna Potter

Making Spaces Safer: A Guide to Giving Harassment the Boot Wherever You Work, Play, and Gather
© 2019 Shawna Potter
This edition © 2019 AK Press (Chico, Edinburgh)

ISBN: 978-1-84935-356-4
E-ISBN: 978-1-84935-357-1
Library of Congress Control Number: 2018961769

AK Press   AK Press
370 Ryan Ave. #100   33 Tower St.
Chico, CA 95973   Edinburgh EH6 7BN
United States   Scotland
www.akpress.org   www.akuk.com
akpress@akpress.org   ak@akedin.demon.co.uk

The above addresses would be delighted to provide you with the latest AK Press distribution catalog, which features books, pamphlets, zines, and stylish apparel published and/or distributed by AK Press. Alternatively, visit our websites for the complete catalog, latest news, and secure ordering

Cover and interior design by Margaret Killjoy
Back cover photo by Chris Sikich
Printed in the USA on acid-free, recycled paper

CONTENTS

INTRODUCTION

I WAS HAVING a good night.

I had traveled to New York City to visit with an old band-mate. Having just moved to the East Coast, my southern self did not think four hours seemed like a long time to drive anywhere, especially for a place that not only had bodegas, but bodegas that stayed open past 9:00 p.m. My friend and I were walking to a subway stop, deep in conversation. It was late, but I felt safe. I could walk down the street at night here and not be scared. There were lights on everywhere, cars were speeding by, people were walking all around. It felt like the city was alive. Aware. I was with a tall guy anyway, so I could relax, right? In my "at ease" state, I felt a hand haphazardly grab and squeeze my butt. The two guys we just passed on the sidewalk were now laughing behind me, quickly walking away. I turned around, stood in place, and yelled at them. "Hey assholes, don't fucking touch me!" More laughs. They were halfway down the block when I said to the two people walking behind them, "You better check your friend, he just fucking grabbed my ass. Tell him that's not cool!" I turned around and started moving, expecting my friend to keep up. I was fuming, complaining loudly about how the entire scene made me feel. After a few moments of silence, this close friend said, "You know, I don't think those people were with those guys. I don't think they knew what you were talking about."

Not "That sucks, I'm sorry" or "What a couple of assholes" or "Drunk fucks; are you alright?" Nothing like that. Frankly, the woman stranger I told to check her "friend" seemed much more concerned about what had just happened than my actual friend. Looking back it feels like his only concern was whether or not I had responded "appropriately" to something wholly inappropriate. While I didn't let being groped that night ruin the rest of my trip, I still think of that moment sometimes. I think it sticks with me because I felt violated, belittled, and alone in the span of five minutes. I wonder if I'd think about it as much if my friend had backed me up. Of course, it's not his fault those guys touched me, but what if he had yelled at them with me, told me I was totally right to call them assholes, or even just given me a hug? Would men who think it's funny to touch a stranger without their permission change their minds if they knew that stranger would have the support of all the people around them?

I have a few car stories, too. The one I often tell when I lead safer space workshops is about the time a guy got out of his car in the middle of an intersection to call me a "cunt" and an "ugly bitch anyway" (among other things) because I had the nerve to absentmindedly flip a middle finger in the air when he honked his car horn at me. That one shook me so hard that I froze until he drove off, and, when I started to walk again, I asked the first friendly person I saw for a hug. The wash of understanding and empathy on the person's face allowed me to let out the tears I had been holding in. I got to share being upset with someone after feeling alone with an angry, reckless man. That is not meant to be poetic. For the full minute he was stopped and yelling at me, that block was deserted. I had no idea if he would run over to me and try to hurt me. I mean, if he was willing to stop and get out of his car in the middle of the street, then what else might he be capable of when a woman makes him angry?

I suppose it's comforting that I get a lot of support from the people taking my workshops, a lot of "That's nuts!" and "I can't believe that guy did that!" or "All that because of a middle finger?" It's obvious to them that his behavior in that moment was wrong. It's also obvious, to me, that their disbelief at this bad behavior, which innocently comes from not experiencing it themselves, could set things up for making someone feel worse about the harassment they just faced. Any statement like "He really did that? Just because you did X?," however well meaning, subtly shifts the focus from his behavior, where it should be, to mine.

Also, disbelief can be read as mistrust. It's hard to hear "I can't imagine why someone would do that" or "I've never seen anything like that," because, well, I have. And so have lots of folks, for various reasons. I might suddenly be wondering if the person I'm telling my story to believes me and will support me, when I should be concentrating on calming down. I've had to lose a giant pickup truck that was following me on my bicycle, making me late for work. I've had to hear someone shout from a car full of men "Can I come over for some pussy later?" and then speed off, as I entered my dad's house while on vacation, not knowing if they lived around there and would, in fact, come back later.

For people who experience harassment often—sexist, racist, homophobic, transphobic, Islamophobic, or ableist— that feeling of "What else is this person capable of?" is common and stressful. It means you're always on guard, waiting for harassment to happen, and knowing, when it does, that it might turn aggressive. All those "minor" instances of harassment can feel pretty major until they are over, because you can't predict the future behavior of someone who is already cool with disrespecting a total stranger.

And each instance matters, because they add up. Those sense memories of feeling isolated and scared compound, making it hard to believe you'll ever go anywhere without being harassed. You've learned to expect it. So much so that even when it doesn't happen, your body has already prepared for it—narrowing your focus, tensing muscles, quickening your breath, and sharpening your mind in case you need to make an emergency decision to maintain your safety. Dealing with harassment is a stressor. According to Harvard Medical School, studies show that "repeated activation of the stress response takes a toll on the body," contributing to high blood pressure as well as mental health concerns like anxiety, depression, and addiction.[1] So while a wolf whistle or a quick shout of "Nice ass!" is not as bad as being groped by a stranger in the middle of the night or being followed by

---

1   "Understanding the Stress Response," *Harvard Mental Health Letter* 27, no. 9 (March 2011): 4–5.

an intimidatingly large vehicle, it's still bad because I don't know if it will get worse. At its least physically draining (but most predictable), it's a mere reminder of all the other times I have been harassed and felt "less than"—like my body doesn't belong to me once I enter a public space; like I'm just a body, not a human being with my own thoughts, dreams, passions, and struggles.

The best way to lessen the feeling of isolation one gets from frequent, commonplace harassment, is to make the response to harassment a group effort. A 2012 study performed by the Worker Institute at Cornell University, reports that:

- When bystanders fail to act, their presence tended to compound targets' negative emotional responses.
- Bystander interventions that had a positive influence on targets could be as simple as a knowing look or a supportive statement.
- When a bystander took action by confronting the harasser, harassment was more likely to stop.[2]

Those last two points are clear, but I want to emphasize the first. When you see harassment happening but do nothing to intervene, it makes the victim feel worse than if dealing with it alone.

---

2   Mary Catt, "Hollaback to Catcalls," *Cornell Chronicle*, May 1, 2012, http://news.cornell.edu/essentials/hollaback-catcalls.

Victim versus Survivor

Not everyone who experiences violence considers themselves a victim. The word "victim" can feel loaded. For some, it seems too serious a designation to describe what they went through, while others don't want to risk being pitied or be seen as helpless. Self-identifying as a "survivor" is a valid way to assert you've come out the other side of a traumatic event, but please know: there is no shame in being a victim. It just means something happened to you that is not your fault. I will mostly be using the word "victim" in this book to describe someone who has experienced harassment or violence based on belonging to a marginalized or oppressed group, but you might also see the terms "survivor" or, to borrow from self-defense language, "target," depending on the context.

The Worker Institute's findings on the effects of bystander intervention were based on descriptions of harassment experiences submitted to the website of Hollaback!, a national organization to end harassment. I founded a Hollaback! chapter in Baltimore in 2011 to address just this problem. After both sitting with these findings for a while and adding basic bystander skills to the Street Harassment 101 workshops I was teaching, two events occurred that made it apparent that a local safer space campaign was not only needed in Baltimore but also that it could make a real difference.

Back in March 2013, our sister group in London shared some inspiring news with the Holla! community. They had just formed a partnership with Fabric, a local nightclub that was tired of hearing secondhand that women were being harassed in their venue. There are many reasons why women and LGBTQIA folks might not report harassment to an establishment's security: fear of victim-blaming, not being taken seriously, possibly experiencing more harassment from typically male staff, and frustration at interrupting their good time to report it are just a few. By going the extra mile and partnering with Hollaback! London, and by pledging to remove harassers from their venue, Fabric showed their community that they prioritize the safety and comfort of their female patrons. Upon hearing this, the Hollaback! team in Baltimore said, "Why not us?"

A few months passed as we considered working on something similar. We then received an inspiring submission on Hollaback! Baltimore's website: The owner of a restaurant called a cab for the victim of transphobic harassment and waited for it with them instead of leaving them alone outside during closing time. After reading a story that so perfectly demonstrated the ideal venue response to harassment, I, my fellow chapter leader Melanie Keller, and our friend and fellow activist Corey Reidy all teamed up to create the Safer Spaces Program in Baltimore. We wanted every restaurant, bar, club, and coffee shop in our town to respond to complaints of harassment in a supportive and consistent way, so that patrons knew what response they'd get when walking into that establishment. I've been training venues on how to best respond to reports of harassment and support people who get harassed in their space ever since. It's essentially highly tailored bystander intervention.

Shawna Potter, Melanie Keller, and Corey Reidy. June 25, 2013.

A few years ago, I needed to step back from my leadership role at Hollaback! in order to devote more attention to my band, War On Women. I've played guitar and been in bands since I was twelve and music is an incredibly important part of my life.

Having stepped back, though, I realized that training venues to become safer spaces was not something I could give up. Nor, as it turned out, did I have to. As I knew from personal experience, music venues can be serious hotbeds of harassment. I could take the Safer Spaces Program on the road, offering trainings to the places where I performed. Through the Entertainment Institute, I was even able to teach safer space tactics to small groups of audience members on the Vans Warped Tour during the summer of 2017. By the end of that summer, I realized I was having nearly identical conversations with attendees, addressing the same questions. My band was performing almost daily on that tour and I was so concerned about saving my voice in order to last the two-month duration that I thought, "What if I just put all this stuff in a book?" That way, next time around, I could save my voice, reach more people, and anyone who read it would be equipped to have those same conversations, too.

As much as I'd love to, it's not logistically or financially feasible for me to personally teach a workshop in every venue around the country, but this information should be in the hands of as many people as possible. I figured it would be much easier and cheaper for venues to read a book and implement what they can. So I wrote one.

My hope for this guidebook is that it can act as a minimum, agreed-upon standard for how every space should operate in order to protect the rights of the people within it to feel physically and mentally safe, supported, and respected. I hope the suggestions are clear and actionable. Where you take it from there is up to you and your community.

Again, what if my friend in New York had had my back? What would I remember from that night then? What if I had never seen a friendly face after being screamed at in broad daylight, and I'd held those tears in? What effect would that have on my body after years and years of harassment? My mind? My confidence in myself? My confidence in others?

On that night ten years ago, I was having a good time. I don't want any more good nights ruined by harassment—for anyone. There will always be assholes, but if you have my back and I have yours, we can face them together. They'll shut up eventually—trust me; we just need to make it clear that they are outnumbered.

Who Is This Book For?

This book is for every house party, basement show, art opening, punk club, community space, library, free farm, sex toy shop, improv group, co-op, coffee shop, piano bar, metal bar, social group, game night, festival, scene, and space where people gather.

Whether you own a space, help run it, work for it, volunteer for it, or just patronize it, this book is for you. Whether you think that space has room for improvement, or if you already love the vibe and just want to keep it, this book is for you. I will tell you now, though: there is always room to improve.

Even if you're not the boss, or your coworkers are not on board, you can still make a huge impact on people's lives by doing everything in this guide that is within your power. No one is ever just an individual. You exist within spaces all the time, and you share some responsibility for what happens there. Your first priority can be everyone's safety, and you can achieve that without cops, violence, or, if you're running a business, any sacrifice to profits—or fun! Cool, right?

Why Safer Spaces?

"One of the foundational parts of building a
community is drawing boundaries about what
is considered acceptable behavior; it's normal
for people to decide that certain actions have no
place in civil society."
—Jessica Valenti, *The Guardian*, June 25, 2018

There is no such thing as an entirely safe space. No one's safety or comfort can be guaranteed 100 percent of the time. This book is about *safer* spaces. However, it's important to point out that, as I use the term, a "safer space" is not one free of challenging ideas or different opinions. It's not about avoiding exposure to people who are different from you. It doesn't even promise that harassment and violence will never happen. But we can always make spaces safer, first by acknowledging that some people are discriminated against just for being who they are, and then by doing what we can to ensure they are believed and supported if it happens on our watch.

The meaning of "safe space" has evolved since the term was first coined. This will likely continue as communities decide for themselves what is or is not acceptable behavior. The concept first arose in the context of "sensitivity training" for corporate management by psychologist Kurt Lewin in the 1940s.[3] As part of a leadership training program developed by Lewin, who founded the National Training Laboratories Institute for Applied Behavioral Sciences, sensitivity training was a form of "group discussion where members could give honest feedback to each other to allow people to become aware of their unhelpful assumptions, implicit biases, and behaviors that were holding them back as effective leaders."[4] The term "safe space" itself is largely reported as gaining traction in the 1960s gay liberation movement and 1970s women's movement. First, gay and lesbian bars served as physically safe spaces where one could behave, dress, and love the way one wanted, out of the public eye. Second, as scholar and activist Moira Kelly writes in her book *Mapping Gay L.A.*, "in the women's movement, [it] was a means rather than an end and not only a physical space but a space created by the coming together of women searching for community."[5] Safe space began to mean "distance from men and patriarchal thought."[6] As the work of Black feminist legal

---

3 Alfred J. Morrow, *The Practical Theorist: The Life and Work of Kurt Lewin* (New York: Basic Books, 1969), 210–214.

4 Vaughn Bell, "The Real History of the 'Safe Space,'" Mind Hacks website, November 12, 2015, https://mindhacks.com/2015/11/12/the-real-history-of-the-safe-space/.

5 Moira Kenny, *Mapping Gay L.A.: The Intersection of Place and Politics* (Philadelphia: Temple University Press, 2001), 24.

6 Malcolm Harris, "What's a 'Safe Space'? A Look at the Phrase's 50-Year History," Splinter News website, November 11, 2015, https://splinternews.com/what-s-a-safe-space-a-look-at-the-phrases-50-year-hi-1793852786.

experts, scholars, and activists became more widely known in the 1980s and '90s, so did the idea that the limitless intersections of identity, and therefore the way people experience harassment and exclusion, could never be perfectly addressed in any space, so *safer* spaces became the more accurate way to describe these efforts. Malcolm Harris explains how these ideas were being put into practice when the term "safe space" hit the mainstream:

> By the time I showed up in left-wing spaces in the early 2000s, that meant horizontal organization and consensus instead of majority rule. It has also meant gender-neutral bathrooms, asking people's preferred pronouns, trigger warnings, internal education "anti-oppression" trainings, and creating separate auxiliary spaces for identity groups to organize their particular concerns. Occupy Wall Street gave these ideas international exposure, but they're not new. Among the likeminded, the "safe space" designation came to signify a set of standard respectful practices.[7]

So this term has gone from describing feeling safe enough to express your opinions without being judged for them, to expressing your true self without fearing violence or arrest, to providing a physical space away from members of your groups' oppressor class, to allowing room to take intellectual risks in order to encourage open dialogue.

---

7   Ibid.

In this book, I want to promote creating physically and emotionally safer spaces. Building upon the work of everyone who has come before, I hope the pages ahead will help take the concept of a safer space out of academia, out of small pockets of alternative or counter culture, and make it something that can thrive anywhere. The idea that everyone should be treated with respect and autonomy should no longer be considered radical. You do not need to be an activist to ensure people have a good time at your venue. It is not overreacting to say "We don't allow hate speech or harassment in this establishment." It is underreacting to let it slide. Besides, who deserves access to true leisure time more? People trying to ruin other people's fun or the people who often get their fun ruined?

What Harassment Looks Like

Harassment can be verbal or physical. It can be based on sex, sexual preferences, gender, religion, race, ability, size, age, class, or any combination of these. It can feel intimidating, hostile, or abusive. Harassing behavior may include name calling, physical assaults or threats, intimidation, ridicule, offensive pictures, and more. It can go from something as simple as being leered at, to being followed in, around, or out of a space. It can be an "accidental" inappropriate touch or an insulting "joke" based on stereotypes. It can be vulgar or offensive slurs mumbled under the breath or yelled out in front of a crowd. It can be a forceful grab over or under clothing, or it can be a forced display of self-manipulation. Most importantly, what someone else would consider harassment might not be harassment for you. You don't need to memorize every potential type of harassment. When someone tells you they were harassed (whether or not they use that word), you just need to remember one thing: believe them.

For the purposes of this book, the harassment we will focus on is the kind that happens in public or semi-public spaces. There are specific protocols and resources available to people experiencing harassment in educational spaces or the workplace, so we'll mostly leave them aside in the pages ahead. In theory, there are more protections at school or work than in other public spaces, but in practice we know that that's not always the case, so feel free to take what we cover here and apply it to any situation, as needed.

Wherever harassment happens, victims are habitually not believed and pushed to remain silent in the hope that the situation will just go away. Simultaneously, systemic racism leads to an imbalance in consequences: people of color, especially Black men, are more likely to face those consequences, and those consequences are likely to be more severe than they are for white people. We don't want to repeat our society's egregious failings by answering one form of injustice with another. We are not here to profile anyone. And, equally, we will not force victims to remain silent. While certain aspects of harassment and safety can be fairly clear-cut—and I'll hopefully be making them clearer in this book—they are embedded in the context of a society that is unjust and unequal in so many ways. That means that we need to operate with honesty and directness. Foregrounding victims—their experiences, their stories, their needs—is an important first step.

This Book Has Grown

Once I had the idea to put the tactics I've been teaching venues into writing, I felt compelled to publish *something* as soon as I could. This information is meant to be shared, and it seemed important to get it out into the world quickly. So, before I wrote the book you're reading, I collected some basic ideas and boiled them down in a small pocket guide that people could easily pass around. AK Press published that in 2018. If you've read that pamphlet, you should be familiar with the some of the basic lessons in this book. If every person at every venue read those tiny forty-eight pages, we'd all have a common language and set of skills to start with as we work to improve our communities and ourselves. This book contains everything in the pocket guide, and it also builds upon it. It goes into more depth than its predecessor, providing more explanations, research, and real-world examples of these tactics in use. Throughout the book you'll also find personal stories, submitted by people with differing responsibilities within their space as well as people who experience harassment, all of which I hope will help illustrate the need for safer spaces in the first place.

As you read, I invite you to think about how everything in this book could apply to you and your space(s). Don't get hung up on any of the terms I choose. When I describe what a space's "owner" can do, feel free to substitute whatever appropriate term applies to your situation and whoever it is that's taking responsibility for how your space operates: employee, volunteer, member, manager, or any other title. What I describe as a "bartender" might be, for you, a different role: security guard, door person, cook, barista, sales associate, or technician. You can substitute "customer" with "patron," "client," "audience," "attendee," "member," or any other term you feel best describes the people being welcomed into the space.

The point is to make this book and the ideas in it your own. I'm thankful that you're reading it in the first place, and I hope you find everything I've added to be helpful.

When Charm City Art Space was offered the chance to be trained and certified as a Safer Space, we jumped at the opportunity. The purpose of CCAS was always to create a space where all were welcome to come and enjoy music, art, and friendly, inclusive people. Becoming a Safer Space meant that we could continue fostering that welcoming environment for people, and if anything happened we would have their back. Thankfully, I only witnessed the need for our training to be put into action a few times—in these cases, CCAS staff was informed that a show attendee felt uncomfortable and/or unsafe based on the actions of another person at the show. When this happened, CCAS staff was able to follow the steps we had learned to take in our Safer Spaces training and resolve the situation. It's not always easy or comfortable to handle these situations or even know what to do, but it's great to have local resources like Hollaback! Baltimore that can inform and guide us to creating a safer community.

—Melanie Losover, former member,
Charm City Art Space

PART I

YOUR SPACE

What you need to create a safer space can be broken up into three categories: obvious intentions, appropriate responses, and accountability. Take away one of these ideas and the others don't work as well. People need to know that they can trust you and your space with their harassment experiences, and you build that trust by responding effectively in the moment as well as owning up to any mistakes or opportunities for improvement.

one

OBVIOUS INTENTIONS

THE REALITY IS that marginalized people experience discrimination in public spaces. As they move through their lives and through various spaces, they cannot predict if they will be treated with respect, let alone if they will be safe. When they attend a show or event at your space, they should be able to know what to expect, or at least what you intend to have happen—and not happen—within your walls. So, how can you let them know? You can't just open the door; you have to put out a welcome mat.

Signs, Online and Off

The first step is making clear what you stand for in every physical and digital space you inhabit. If you have clear wording on your website, social media, flyers, event pages, menus, entryways, bathrooms, et cetera, people will know that "Harassment and Violence Will Not Be Tolerated" or that yours is a "Hate-Free Zone." I encourage you to get specific about what you don't tolerate and how you'll handle it by posting an official "Anti-Harassment Policy" on your website and the walls of your space. You can find more examples of these in the appendix.

Your messaging should make it clear that staff will take complaints of harassment seriously and that harassers will be dealt with appropriately. This is good for potential victims to know, as well as potential harassers.

Once you've let people know that the staff is on their side, you have to let them know who the staff is. Designate who can handle their questions and complaints by having people wear a "Staff" shirt, sash, button, hat, apron, or hoodie. You have options, so whether you all agree to wear the same color or use the space's name or logo, your patrons should know who they can trust when something happens.

Remember, there's more than one sort of harassment, even though our society might discuss some more than others. For instance, is your space trans-friendly? Say so! Make your restroom signage obvious and clear: toilets or urinals, sitting or standing, single stall for everyone, or whatever your set-up is. Just make sure people know they can use whichever bathroom they feel most comfortable in with the full support of staff.

There are also important class and accessibility issues every space must consider when it comes to events. Let people know about sliding scale donations, the closest public transportation stops, and ramp availability (or lack thereof) on all flyers and event pages.

Share your awesome policies online from time to time as a reminder to your community. This is easily done and can be scheduled in advance. Who knows? Maybe making these things part of public discourse might inspire other spaces to do the same.

Finally, it's crucial to provide a way for folks to communicate with you anonymously with any complaints or suggestions. This is so they can do so without fear of retribution. Set up an anonymous message form on your site, provide an email address dedicated to complaints of harassment, or, if they want to mail it in, let people know to whose attention they should address it.

Make Your Space Welcoming for All

Dealing with harassment itself means that the problem has already happened, but you can go a long way toward *preventing* harassment if respect is built into your space and its various elements. When you do the work to make it clear that everyone is welcome, it becomes part of the overall atmosphere.

People have different needs. When you anticipate people's needs before they arrive, it shows that you acknowledge that they exist and that you value having them in your space. If you don't have some particular accommodation and you've found a workaround for it, display obvious signage to let people know. I've created a few checklists to start you thinking about how to build a welcoming space. Check off the ones you already have. Some of the accommodations listed below are required by the Americans with Disabilities Act. Since state laws can vary as long as they don't directly conflict with the federal law, it's important for a manager or owner to know what exactly is required in each state. But you're not doing all this just to avoid litigation, right? You're doing it because you want people to feel welcome. I encourage you to exceed legal requirements and even people's expectations. I've left a few spaces blank so you can add some items specific to your space.

Accessibility

- ☐ A ramp or alternative path for each set of stairs.
- ☐ A bathroom stall that can fit someone's wheelchair.
- ☐ A spot to watch the show from a seated position.
- ☐ A couple of extra chairs (not bar stools) with no arm rests so it's easy to get in and out of them.
- ☐ Menus in Braille.
- ☐ Paper and pen available for people who cannot hear or speak (or, better yet, someone who knows ASL).
- ☐ If you have a signer for your event, include a "Sign Language Interpreter" symbol on all flyers and advertisements. An online image search will give you plenty of options.
- ☐ Free and easy-to-obtain water.
- ☐ A warning for intense light shows, the use of strobe lights, or smoke machines.
- ☐ _____
- ☐ _____
- ☐ _____

Food Options[1]

☐ Staff members who all know the difference between an intolerance and an allergy.

☐ Options available for the most common allergens and dietary restrictions.

☐ Protocols in place to keep problematic ingredients separated, when prepared and stored.

☐ EpiPens (for people with severe allergies) on-site that everyone knows how to use.

☐ _____

☐ _____

☐ _____

Gender

☐ Gender-affirming or -neutral language on bathroom signage.

☐ Bag hooks in the bathroom stalls and at the bar.

☐ Toilet paper, paper towels, and soap in the bathroom.

☐ Obvious signage that transphobia or transphobic language is not allowed.

☐ _____

☐ _____

☐ _____

Of course, making safer spaces is more than a checklist. You have to think both holistically and specifically. For instance, don't overlook the little things that make up the

---

1 You can find information regarding your state's laws and more through FARE: Food Allergy Research and Education.

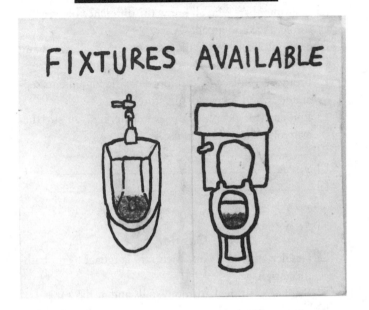

FIXTURES AVAILABLE

overall feel of your space. Don't give a pass to discriminatory statements, art, or "jokes" on event flyers, tip jars, or band merchandise. What you allow says something about your space. This includes the break room and other employee-only areas. Taking this seriously when no customers are looking makes it easier for staff to take customers seriously when they voice their concerns.

How about the resources specific to your town? Keep the numbers for taxis, shelters, and local support hotlines available at your door, front desk, or office. Have multiple copies on hand, especially if you have a bar, back room, or an upstairs. This book includes a list of national hotline numbers in the appendix, as well as room to fill in your local numbers.

Have a first aid kit on hand. Offer condoms and tampons, with signage in the bathrooms to let people know where or from whom to get them. And while there is not much a dive bar can do about the "old beer and fresh bleach" smell, other types of venues can go scent-free for those with fragrance sensitivities.

Naloxone, also known as Narcan, is a medication used to prevent overdoses by blocking the effects of opioids. You could save a life by having the pocket-sized injector or nasal spray on hand.

Can you think of any more considerations? List them below and check off the ones you have put into action so far.

- ☐ _____
- ☐ _____
- ☐ _____
- ☐ _____
- ☐ _____

Get Everyone on Board

If no one has your back when it comes to making your workplace safer, the way you interact with and support patrons can still have a huge impact them, so keep it up! You can't make it an "official safer space," though, if you're the only one who knows about the improvements you've made. In other words, unless the entire venue is on board, you'll never reach everyone in your community who needs a safer space. So take it one day at a time. Chip away at the barriers that keep your colleagues from embracing these policies. Tell them about what you are getting out of this guidebook, your success stories, and how doing good makes you feel good. At the very least, you'll be the resident anti-harassment figure who everyone can (inevitably) turn to.

When I used to run house shows in London, my way of trying to make them a safer space was to point out that they were happening in a kitchen, with a gas hob, and that any sexist, racist, transphobic, homophobic, or generally shit behaviour could lead to you being set on fire. Half-joking aside, I had to fight so hard, alongside other women, to make that punk house a slightly safer space. I was sexually assaulted there a number of times, including once by a guy who came all the way up the stairs into my bedroom and got into my bed to touch me up whilst I was asleep. It took me years to get him to be accountable for that. And so many other things happened that I haven't got the time or energy to challenge, especially now that it's not an active gig space anymore.

We need safer spaces to make it easier for everyone to organise politically, and also for us all to have a fucking break sometimes. I am so grateful for all the work that has been done to challenge sexual harassment and assault at gigs because I'm starting to relax and feel like I can let my guard down—and this is important for being able to recharge, to keep fighting.

—Ren Aldridge, Petrol Girls/Nasty Women

Common Concerns and How to Address Them

I'm not saying it will be easy. Dealing with harassment can be uncomfortable. You're asking your staff or coworkers to step up, be a little courageous. That might not be something they're used to, and our patriarchal culture has plenty of ready-made excuses and ways to avoid facing the reality of harassment. You'll definitely have to deal with some of them.

"I don't wanna talk about it." Sometimes people think the way to get rid of a problem is to not talk about it, that silence around tough issues will make them go away. This isn't true, of course. In fact, it often makes the situation worse. Tension can build, resentment sets in, and people will give up and leave your space rather than risk a conversation with someone who seems unwilling to hear them. So ask your staff or coworkers to flip the script. When customers approach them about harassment or discrimination, it is not a nuisance. It's an opportunity to make them feel safe and valued. Which, presumably, will ensure a return visit from the people you want returning—otherwise the only people you'll have left in your space will be the ones harassing.

"What about the men?" A safer space is just a place where people feel comfortable being themselves. This is achieved by supporting people, encouraging them to speak up, listening, and ultimately taking action when they feel threatened or intimidated. Spaces where white cisgender men can feel comfortable being and expressing themselves—and where they are sure to be taken seriously—are abundant. Spaces where people who are not white cisgender men are afforded that same respect and consideration are not. That's why it takes a little bit more work to provide that space and ensure that people know about it.

Society has historically given the benefit of the doubt to men who perpetrate violence while constantly questioning the women and LGBTQIA people who file complaints of harassment or reports of sexual assault, regardless of a mountain of harrowing statistics showing they're telling the truth. Two-thirds of women in the United States have experienced street harassment at some point in their lives, and 68 percent of those women were concerned that it would escalate into something more violent.[2] A 2012 survey conducted of gay and bisexual men in the United States also found that 90 percent reported being harassed or made to feel unwelcome in public spaces because of their sexual orientation.[3] Approximately one in five women in the United States have been victims of rape, and half of all women have been victims of other forms of sexual violence at some point in their lives.[4] Moreover, men are far more likely to be victims of rape themselves than they are to be falsely accused of rape; 1.4 percent of men in the United States reported being raped in

---

2   Holly Kearl, Unsafe and Harassed in Public Spaces: A National Street Harassment Report (Reston, VA: Stop Street Harassment, 2014), http://www.stopstreetharassment.org/our-work/nationalstudy.

3   Patrick McNeil, "Harassing Men on the Street." *Feministe*. October 15, 2012.

4   M.C. Black, et al., *The National Intimate Partner and Sexual Violence Survey (NISVS): 2010 Summary Report.* (Atlanta: National Center for Injury Prevention and Control, 2011), 18.

their lifetime.[5] Of the 32 percent of all rapes that are actually reported, about 2–10 percent are false accusations.[6]

It's not a zero-sum game. Intentionally and publicly supporting women and LGBTQIA folks, in addition to following through upon receiving complaints of harassment, doesn't make a space less safe for men—it makes it more fun for everyone.

"That's never happened here." *That you know of.* If people don't trust you to take their stories of harassment seriously, then they won't tell you when it happens. Maybe one of your other staff members harassed them before. Maybe there is sexist, transphobic, or racist imagery on display (old posters, flyers, stickers, the shirt the bartender is wearing). Maybe they overheard your coworkers' "joke," and it did not come off well. Maybe they never told anyone at your venue about that time they were harassed and left because of it, merely because they had been disbelieved, silenced, or ignored whenever they'd told their story in the past. You won't stand a chance of gaining their trust without putting down the welcome mat and making it obvious your venue has their back. When I train venues to become official safer spaces, it's common for me to warn them that they might see an uptick in reported stories. It's not that harassment is happening more, it's just that your patrons are more willing to trust you with their stories. That's a good thing.

---

5   Ibid., 26.

6   D. Lisak, et al., "False Allegations of Sexual Assault: An Analysis of Ten Years of Reported Cases," *Violence Against Women* 16, no. 12 (December 2010): 1330.

Hiring and Curating Events without Bias

Marginalized people feel more comfortable around people who are like them. Prioritize hiring people from a variety of backgrounds and life experiences. Pay people fairly and equally—white men do not get to make more for doing the same job! Some businesses opt for transparency by publicly posting the pay rate for each job, preventing the internal biases of the person doing the hiring from affecting the person being hired.

If you are only booking straight, white, cis male bills, artists and audiences will notice, and they will be increasingly more vocal about it when they do. Sometimes it takes extra work or a financial risk to book new or unknown artists who do not fit the patriarchal mold, but it must be done, and the more it's done, the easier it is to keep doing it. When diversity is expected by audiences, everyone in your scene knows that they would be welcome on that club stage or gallery wall, giving you more bands and artists to choose from in the future! Strive to never have an event that only features straight, white, cisgender men. Linda Holmes, host of NPR's *Pop Culture Happy Hour*, has a great perspective on curating diverse bills:

> The reason you have to be aware of whether your shows are inclusive is not because women otherwise aren't good enough. It's because you, as a curator, have antennae that are naturally more likely to hear some voices than others. That's true, in my opinion, of basically everyone…. Your effort is to compensate for your own limitations, not to compensate

for other people's not being able to compete. And those limitations aren't necessarily because you're a bad person! Two equally aware, thoughtful people can have totally different references. I am much more likely to naturally notice things that vibrate on a frequency that thrums in my head, but as a curator, I can't confuse that with quality or meritocracy. So if you don't notice gender, if you "don't see color"...? You'll perpetuate your own limits.[7]

Of course, even the best curator or booker can't know everything about every act or artist they schedule. What if you're caught off guard and a featured band or performer is causing problems by being sexist, homophobic, or racist? This scenario is bound to happen. It's often outside your control, especially if you're *not* the person doing the booking. There are still ways to demonstrate the "obvious intentions" of your space, to both restrict their platform and show your patrons that you don't support that bullshit. You can turn on the house lights when they make offensive remarks, or simply turn off the sound to cut their set short. Cut them off at the bar. Wear a shirt or make a sign at the door or on the tip jar that says you don't stand by their remarks or beliefs, or even that just says what you *do* believe in (as in, "Black Lives Matter," "Believe Victims," "Refugees Welcome Here"). You can get creative with it or simply go with a classic "Booooo!" instead of applause. When you assert your values, you empower others to do the same—and you do it on behalf

---

7   Linda Holmes (@lindaholmes), Twitter posts, October 3, 2017.

of those who, for whatever reason, still don't feel powerful enough to do it themselves.

There was a situation where a specific show was happening with a known abuser in one of the bands. Since the venue was trained by Hollaback! Baltimore and was a safer space, I knew that the employees would take my concerns seriously, even if their conclusion wouldn't be what I had hoped. In the end, they removed the band from the show.

—Chris Belkas, Fake Crab Records

Policies for Those First Crucial Moments

The more you can do in advance to help people feel safe in your space, the better their experience. Obvious signage, a knowledgeable and diverse staff, and inclusive shows are all positive steps toward that goal. Unfortunately, it does not mean harassment and violence will never occur in your space. You need clear, actionable policies in place before an incident occurs, so that things don't go off the rails in the very first moments. Chapter 2 will go into this in more detail and give you the raw material to devise your own robust and extensive plan for responding to ugly behavior in your space, but let's establish some foundations of care. This will minimize any missteps or time wasted.

The short version is this: you and your staff need to be able to ground people who are in crisis and avoid victim-blaming.

And you need to know in advance how to do or not do these things. That's what makes it a policy.

First of all, not everything is a crisis, but you should definitely know when it is. A crisis is defined by three key things: (1) a high level of stress is present, (2) the person finds it difficult or impossible to cope, and (3) it is temporary.

Responses to crisis may vary, but some people may be sobbing, yelling, taking very short breaths, or speaking too fast. On the other hand, they could be very quiet, staring into space, and nonresponsive. This is because they have temporarily lost their coping skills. If someone cannot relate their story to you effectively, they may be in "crisis mode" and unless they can be brought back into the present moment, or *grounded*, then you won't be able to help them.

Therefore, before we get into the details in Chapter 2, let's talk about how to deal with someone in crisis. That way, even if you only read this chapter, you'll be much better off—and more helpful. After all, people can experience a loss of coping skills after *any* traumatic event, so by memorizing the techniques below—and training others to do the same—you'll be ready assist no matter the situation. The techniques are the same for all sorts of crises: harassment, assault, or rape; a robbery or theft; a car accident; a mass shooting event; a hate crime; the effects of military assaults (on soldiers and civilians); and even unexpected events that trigger memories of previous traumas, like a particular phrase or smell or object connected to the original event, or seeing similar situations played out on a national scale in the twenty-four-hour news cycle.

If you believe someone is in crisis, your first priority is to help them feel as grounded as they can given the situation. Some common grounding techniques:

- Take deep breaths. Ask the person if they will take five deep breaths with you and then start to exhibit the breathing, saying "Breathe in ... Okay, now, breathe out ... Okay, let's do it again, breathe in ... good." How many of you took a deep breath just reading this? Once you start, the other person's body should naturally start to copy your breathing. It's very contagious and a great way to regulate someone's heartbeat.

- Say five things you see, five things you hear, and five things you feel. This requires sitting still and focusing on present surroundings. It is difficult for the brain to do this while also living in the crisis. So have them get specific. If they fall silent, keep asking "Yeah, what else?"

- Have them say the following: "I am [their name]. I am sitting in a chair [standing, etc.] I am safe right now." Repeat as needed.

- Take off your shoes and rub your feet on the ground. This one might not be appropriate in some settings, so be mindful of actions that could be "too intimate." For example, unless someone reaches out for a hug, or you've asked "do you need a hug?" and they give a positive response, try to avoid touching them unnecessarily.

Once someone is able to tell you what has happened or how you can help, let them! No need to keep talking about breathing. And if you read the situation wrong and they say "Why do I need to breathe? The jerk is over there, are you gonna talk to them or what?" just quickly apologize and move on to helping them.

While you're grounding someone, be warm and empathetic and *listen* to them. Validate their feelings by using phrases such as "I believe you," "It's not your fault," and "You have the right to be safe in this venue." It will help the victim and at the same time will help you avoid a common problem they often face: victim-blaming.

What Is Victim-Blaming?

When approached by someone who has experienced harassment, *being their advocate is your number one priority*. Incidents of harassment unfold within a particular society. In our case, that's a society defined by a range of unequal power relations. That means that those with power—the abusers—often get to control the narrative that describes their own actions and those of the abused. The result is a cultural bias that blames people for their own victimization. It is of the utmost importance to recognize what victim-blaming is and to avoid it.

Victim-blaming is when the victim of a crime is held partially or completely responsible for what happened to them. This occurs far too often in cases of rape, sexual assault, and harassment. Victim-blaming is dangerous because it wrongfully focuses attention and fault on someone who has done nothing wrong and takes attention *off of* those who have. It also re-traumatizes victims and prevents them from coming forward to report crime for fear of retribution, judgment, and scrutiny from the authorities, family, friends, and society as a whole.

Why Do People Victim-Blame?

The benefit of blaming the victim for those who harass and assault is obvious: they're let off the hook. Unfortunately, they're not the only ones who do it. Victim-blaming distances people—especially the most vulnerable—from fully processing an awful occurrence by reinforcing the popular belief that crimes, like harassment, are infrequent and only happen to people who are careless. People reassure themselves, "Because I wear this and act in that way, what happened to that person will never happen to me." This is simply not true. Moreover, it's a very dangerous misconception that makes things worse. The truth of the matter is that *most* individuals belonging to a marginalized population have experienced harassment based on their identity (or identities or perceived identities), and the key to ending it isn't blaming the people who suffer the effects of abusive behavior but holding people who abuse accountable for said behavior.

So there you have it. You've done all the preparation you need to do, or enough to feel confident. Now comes the time to understand that all the preparation in the world can't guarantee anything. Chapter 2 will be your training in what to do when the behaviors you hoped to avoid have happened anyway. We're in this for the long haul, building a better world inch by difficult inch. Until that new day dawns, we'll still have a lot of messes to clean up.

two

APPROPRIATE RESPONSES

As SHOULD BE clear by now, appropriate responses to harassment must be victim-centered. That means we must prioritize the desires, safety, and well-being of the person suffering harassment in every aspect of our response. It means we need to protect a victim's privacy and personal boundaries and only take our response in the direction they want us to take it. Underlying all this is an attitude that should be obvious but that always bears repeating: the victim of harassment is *never* responsible for the abusive behavior they've experienced.

Being victim-centered also requires a sort of informed empathy that takes into account the physical and psychological effects of harassment. These effects are real. They are ongoing, cumulative, and *traumatic*.

Of course we want our response to harassment to be appropriate, but appropriate to what exactly? For marginalized groups, no act of abuse is isolated: they have most likely suffered through such situations many times in the past. The particular act of harassment you are responding to may seem large or small, egregious, or simply unthoughtful. However it looks, you can be sure that it's the tip of an ugly iceberg. A lifetime of harassment takes its toll, and this can affect how victims experience and react to oppressive behavior. Understanding this is important. It also means understanding the nature of trauma.

The Effects of Trauma

The word "trauma" can be used to describe both something that causes psychological pain or damage and that pain or damage itself. What really defines it, though—and this goes all the way back to Freud—is the fact that the traumatic event causes "emotions that overwhelm the psyche and produce psychological aftereffects."[1] It's a very normal and automatic response to an abnormal event. The overwhelming nature of the trauma means that it can't be processed or integrated like mundane memories, so the experience can remain present, raw, and unhealed.

Violence and harassment (which often carries an underlying threat of violence) can be traumatic. In turn, posttraumatic stress disorder (PTSD) can develop from direct or indirect exposure to something traumatic, or from repeated exposure to *elements* of something traumatic. Whether we are

---

1 I. Lisa McCann and Laurie Anne Pearlman, *Psychological Trauma and Adult Survivor Theory: Therapy and Transformation* (London: Routledge, 2015), 46.

the one being attacked or seeing it happen to others, we can experience elements of PTSD in response. It can even occur after putting up with repeated microaggressions like common street harassment that, on their own, don't seem so bad but that remind us of previous traumas. National estimates of exposure to traumatic events reveal that women are more likely to be diagnosed with PTSD than men. There are some sad statistics about this from the Rape, Abuse, and Incest National Network, including the fact that "94% of women who are raped experience symptoms of post-traumatic stress disorder (PTSD) during the two weeks following the rape" and "30% of women report symptoms of PTSD 9 months after the rape."[2]

In addition to gender-related abuse, "overall, African Americans have a 9.1% prevalence rate for PTSD, compared to 6.8% in Whites."[3] In "The Link Between Racism and PTSD," Monnica T. Williams argues that "the unpredictable and anxiety-provoking nature of [racism-related experiences], which may be dismissed by others, can lead to victims feeling as if they are 'going crazy.' Chronic fear of these experiences may lead to constant vigilance or even paranoia, which over time may result in traumatization or contribute to PTSD when a more stressful event occurs later."[4]

Considering that one in every six American women is said to have been the victim of attempted or completed rape, that's

2   "Victims of Sexual Violence: Statistics," Rape, Abuse, and Incest National Network, https://www.rainn.org/statistics/victims-sexual-violence.

3   Monnica T. Williams, "The Link Between Racism and PTSD," *Psychology Today*, September 6, 2015, https://www.psychologytoday.com/us/blog/culturally-speaking/201509/the-link-between-racism-and-ptsd.

4   Ibid.

a lot of people walking around with PTSD or its symptoms, and that's not including everyone else who's been a victim of hate speech, hate violence, or identity-based attacks. A key component of discrimination in our culture is that it minimizes the very real suffering of marginalized people. We're made to think they are overreacting, that they *want* to play the victim or just love drama.

It takes less effort to dismiss victims than to advocate for them, so these responses can be hard to unlearn. An average person, even one who might want to help, can find it frustrating when a victim's story is "all over the place" or if they can't remember every detail about what happened. Conversely, we might question the validity of someone's claims because they just don't seem "that upset." This line of thinking can be corrected by understanding more about how the brain works. Let's break down what the brain is doing when it senses potential danger.

Remember my story of freezing up when a man got out of his car to yell at me? That was not the first time I had ever been harassed. I have been touched without my permission (by men and women), I've had strange men yell at me for not smiling at their "compliments," and I've had men talk about my body parts and what they'd like to do with them. I've seen countless movies and television shows that make being attacked or raped seem inevitable, and I've heard tons of anecdotes from friends, family, and colleagues about the violence they've endured at the hands of men. Collectively and over time, all of this seems to imply that, as a woman, I am in danger from men at all times, that I'm only safe from their violence if *they* choose to let me be. It sounds paranoid, even to me, but these are the unconscious lessons I've been learning since even before hitting puberty.

When that man honked his car horn, I felt emboldened to put a middle finger in the air because my amygdala, which is the part of the brain always scanning the environment for threats, found none. Everything in my experience indicated that the car would keep driving and I would keep walking. It was when I heard those tires screech to a quick halt that my amygdala set off an alarm of fear, telling the rest of my mind "Protect us now!"

This is where it gets interesting: the prefrontal cortex (the center of higher thought) is a more complicated and advanced part of the brain. It's more "aware," so it's a little slower to react than the amygdala, which is an older and more automatic part of the brain. After the fear alarm is set off, the hippocampus stops filing memories and focuses on pumping cortisol to help the body not feel pain, in preparation for a potential fight. In essence, the prefrontal cortex is no longer in charge, making it more difficult to process what is happening while it's happening. At that point one is most likely relying on learned, ingrained behavior, which doesn't always look like the right response to an event.[5]

In my case, I froze. What the mind does to protect the body might not seem logical in hindsight, and in reality it can get in the way of "gathering evidence" after the fact (as

---

5   J. Douglas Bremner, *Does Stress Damage the Brain: Understanding Trauma-Related Disorders from a Mind Body Perspective* (New York: W.W. Norton, 2002), 132–133. See also J. Douglas Bremner, "Traumatic Stress: Effects on the Brain," *Dialogues in Clinical Neuroscience* 8, no. 4 (December 2006): 445–461.

the Senate confirmation of frat-boy judge Brett Kavanaugh to the Supreme Court perhaps made clear in the autumn of 2018). Since memory filing has been interrupted, logical, linear stories are not likely directly after a traumatic event, and pushing for one will not help ground the victim (more on that later). Service providers who work with victims of assault and rape are usually advised to engage with memories in whatever order they come and not worry about the timeline when trying to learn what happened. After focusing on sense memories, asking open-ended follow-up questions can help the victim relate the events that took place in a chronological order.

Also, repeated abuse makes trauma symptoms worse. Think about how common it is to see a dog who's been beaten repeatedly in the past cower when it hears a loud noise. That dog might even stay on guard when its owner is not overtly happy—just in case. We all do our own version of staying on guard after experiencing any level of violence.

What does all this have to do with creating safer spaces? We have to let go of the idea that there is a "perfect victim" or a correct way to act after a traumatic experience. The research shows otherwise. Self-protection habits include the commonly known "fight, flight, or freeze" as well as the lesser-known "Friend" (also sometimes called "Fawn," this is the strategy of turning on the charm to befriend and "disarm" an attacker, something we learn to do as smiling infants). Fight and flight are self-explanatory, but when freezing continues, it can become immobility in the form of temporary paralysis, muscle rigidity, or loss of consciousness. One can even go into a dissociative state, feeling blank and disconnected from the body, like going on autopilot. Obviously, this is not the same as "letting something happen," and it's just as valid a response as fighting back.

"Secondary victimization" refers to the retraumatization that can occur when someone encounters insensitive or victim-blaming authority figures like police, security, or staff. It can compound the effects of the original trauma. "Why didn't you tell anyone at the time?"—a fear of statements like this can discourage victims from seeking any assistance in the moment. If they once felt that the person they shared their story with didn't believe them—and perhaps even harassed them further—in the future they might not risk telling anyone at all. So, at best, they leave a space to avoid the situation, and at worst they stick around and suffer through someone following them around or making derogatory comments to them all night.

That's why there are some standards when dealing with someone who's been through any kind of trauma (such as harassment, car crash, or witnessing something intense). We'll go over how to incorporate this knowledge in a venue-specific way later, but generally speaking, when working with victims there are a few key things to keep in mind:

- Give them a voice and a choice (ask them where would they like to sit, if they want water, etc.).
- Make sure they not only are physically safe enough to talk with you, but also that they *feel* physically safe enough. Give them a little privacy or move them away from prying eyes.
- Provide transparency. Tell them what is about to happen, and then follow through. This would mean, for instance, telling them if you are about to ask a series

of questions or going to get a manager, if you need to leave them alone, and, if so, when you will be back.

- Collaborate with them on any future plans. Don't tell them what they have to do, instead let them know their options and ask them what might work better for them. If they aren't sure yet, you can even say, "Most people in your position might choose to…" This still lets them have the final say. This might include crafting a safety plan or listing their next steps for the coming forty-eight hours.

- Finally, keep cultural issues in mind. Maybe you're not the best person to help the victim in this moment. If you represent the same oppressor group as the person who caused the victim harm, you might want to enlist the help of someone who looks like the victim, who can immediately provide a sense of camaraderie. Use your best judgment.

When you give trauma-informed care (or victim-centered care), it prevents secondary traumatization, allowing everyone to deal with the original incident more effectively. It also empowers the victim, perhaps giving them the courage, or at least the option, of not putting up with harassment in the future but instead enlisting the aid of others.

It's Time to Walk the Walk

Okay. So now you've got some policies in place and your signage posted. You have a basic idea about what someone who has endured harassment or assault might be going through. You're ready for everyone to show up and have a great time, right? Fantastic! Now comes the real work: being ready to handle incidents of harassment and violence in real time *in a victim-centered way* that does not escalate the situation.

This might seem obvious, but let's break it down. If you are going to advertise that you are a safer space, you'd better be one. Posters are great, but the real work is done in the moment, when someone trusts you enough to say "I was just harassed." By handling these moments appropriately, you positively impact how the victim processes the incident when it's all over, and you ensure continued trust. Your actions also send a message to any would-be creeps about what sort of behavior is acceptable on your watch. Who knows? Maybe you also inspire a bystander or two to understand that an effective and appropriate response is possible.

The remainder of this chapter guides you through the basics of how to address harassment in your space, based on the Safer Spaces Program I helped create in Baltimore. As you read, think about how you can apply these ideas to your unique space. These techniques become easier and feel more natural with repetition, so practice them with friends or coworkers.

Listen, Act, Check In

Let's make something clear from the outset: you are not a cop, a counselor, or a judge. You are not there to take a testimony or find someone guilty. You aren't trained to give on-the-spot therapy. You are playing a limited role: one human being helping another through a bad situation. You are only there to support the victim by validating their experience and doing what is reasonably within your power to help them feel safe. By the time they come to you, it's past the point of being something they can just brush off. It's also possible it has happened to other people that same night. You need to take it seriously, and, as we touched on in chapter 1, that starts with listening.

> *I feel that talking to the victim is the most important aspect of a safer space. When it comes down to it, I think that, while there is room to allow a harasser to learn from their mistakes, many of them are given a pass or even groomed by society in their behavior. Providing a victim with someone to talk to, especially someone who has tools to help them through their situation, is a vital element in a safer space. This also hopefully creates an environment where people would feel comfortable coming to anyone in the collective if they had a concern around a particular person or show.*
>
> —Chris Belkas, former member,
> Charm City Art Space

Listen

First and most importantly: believe the victim.

When you do that, it's easier to listen to them and concentrate on validating their experience. There are dozens of books out there on "active listening" so if this is a challenge for you, you might want to read one—or five. Your job here is to build understanding and trust. Make gentle eye contact, nod your head, and echo their language (this repeats what they are trying to express back to them and lets them know you hear them). Acknowledge that you're sorry they experienced something that made them feel unsafe, thank them for telling you, and assure them that since yours is a safer space, you'll handle the situation so they can keep enjoying their time.

Okay, that's the best-case scenario. What if they are unable to tell you what's going on? Unresponsive or sobbing uncontrollably? They might be in crisis. When someone is in "crisis mode" they are not in the present moment with you. They are reliving a past trauma, the one that just happened or, more likely, that one compounded by older, similar experiences, large and small. You need them to communicate with you in order for you to help them, so you'll need to get them back to the present. If you need to, go back and look at the grounding techniques discussed in chapter 1. A tactic I didn't mention there is asking the victim to describe one object in the room in great detail. By focusing on one tangible thing so intensely, the brain can't also focus on negative thoughts.

The basic elements of meditation can also be employed here, in a condensed form. As Amanda Schupak has pointed out, a mere two minutes of focusing on your breath and your surroundings can effectively reduce anxiety.[6] It's an effective tactic whether someone has been harassed, was just in a car accident, or is having a panic attack.

Keep in mind, though, it's important to avoid touching someone in crisis unless they reach out for you. Be aware of power dynamics in these situations. Your intentions don't matter as much as their perceptions of such dynamics. As I

6   Amanda Schupak, "Here's an Easy 2-Minute Trick to Calm Your Racing Mind," *Self*, January 28, 2016, https://www.self.com/story/trick-to-stop-racing-thoughts.

suggested above, if they were just assaulted by someone who looks like you, you might not be the best person to calm them down.

If someone is not really in crisis, but they are upset, you always have the option of offering to talk with them in a more private, quiet space. Or offer to let them sit down next to you for a minute until they're ready to talk. Offer them water. Give them a little time and assure them that you're here to help.

Act

Now that you've made sure the victim is not still in crisis mode and you've actively listened to them, you can take action. For the program I run, we teach people to give the victim three options. It's empowering for them to decide how they want the situation handled. Your choices will have to be limited to actions you can realistically take, but, even so, giving someone an immediate sense of control over their fate can be incredibly helpful. Even if they don't feel it necessary for action to be taken (sometimes people just want to be heard), it helps them to feel safe knowing you were willing to take action. Also, three options are easy for everyone to remember!

"I can keep an eye on the person." This is the simplest option—at least in terms of what you need to do initially. It means exactly what it says: you will watch the person who has been pointed out to you for the remainder of the event. However, this is not an excuse to profile people of color or make someone uncomfortable who might already feel unwelcome. You will continue to provide the same good service to this alleged harasser, just like you would a bad tipper or close-talker. Just as you were when dealing with the person who was harassed, you need to keep a level head and stay grounded in the here and now, not in who this possible harasser might be or what they might do. The accusation is just something to keep in mind in case the bad behavior repeats or gets worse.

"I can talk to the person." Assure the victim you'll wait until the coast is clear before speaking to the alleged harasser so you don't betray their privacy. Approach the harasser calmly and politely, letting them know that the behavior in question is not cool in your space. It's fine to give them the benefit of the doubt, let them know someone "interpreted" their behavior in a creepy or threatening way, and you are just giving them a heads-up so they don't "accidentally" do it again. Focus on the behavior, not the person. By giving them an out and allowing them to save face, you decrease the chances of escalating the situation. End it by pointing to your policy on the wall (because you already have one by now, right?) and telling them where you'll be all night if they need anything or have any questions. This subtly lets them know you will be keeping an eye on them and that they cannot repeat their inappropriate behavior and expect to be allowed to stay.

"I can kick the person out." This option takes more nerve on your part, but a space that doesn't offer this choice is "safer" in name only. You're being victim-centered, remember? That means you do what you can to meet the needs of the person who has been violated. That should also include not escalating the situation, for the victim's sake and yours. You can say something like: "You're not banned for life, but you gotta go now. You did something against our safer space policy, so I have to ask you to leave." If you need to, you can always offer to refund their money, call them a cab, whatever. Just stay calm and get them outside and on their way. Most spaces I train automatically go to this option if someone has been inappropriately touched without consent, just like they would for any overtly offensive act. It's a serious enough accusation that you might feel an obligation, as a space, to remove the accused immediately to protect all your patrons.

If your space has this automatic ejection policy, you need to gently make this clear to the victim. Use grounding techniques if necessary, avoid victim-blaming language, believe, validate, and listen to them. Then you can say, "That's totally unacceptable behavior here, so I'm gonna go handle this and make sure they leave. In the meantime, do you want to sit over here/grab a friend/hang out in the office till I get back? Okay, cool, I'll come check on you again once they are gone, okay?" Then, *follow through*: come back to check on them, knowing that they might need to tell you their story one more time.

If you are not the person who kicks people out, that's fine. Stay with the victim and delegate the ejecting to the right folks. The same is true if you're not the designated listener. You still say the above, just change it to "I'm gonna go handle this; while I'm gone would you be cool sitting with Mel, our bartender? Yeah? Hey, Mel, can you come here? Lisa here has had a rough night, can you just get her whatever she needs? Water, a friendly ear, a chair? Great, okay, I'll come check on you later." Our fictional Mel is probably a warm, caring person who quickly understands that her role is to just be there. When you come back to check on them, just keep it simple: "Just wanted to tell you that person is gone for the night. Whatever you need from us, if you want to sit for a while or want us to walk you to your car when you leave, or if you want to report the incident, just let Mel know; we'll be happy to do whatever we can to help you out. Again, so sorry this happened, and I just want to thank you again for telling us so we could deal with it." This way, you follow through, keep in communication with the victim about what is going on, but make it clear that you are not her point person.

However you proceed, it's not a bad idea to let another co-worker or volunteer know you're about to approach an alleged harasser. They can look out for you if the situation escalates or keep an eye on the person when you inevitably leave to use the bathroom or get caught up in another task. It also feels good to know you're not on your own. When you do have someone to watch your back when you approach a harasser, have them stay at a distance—otherwise it's too intimidating and can seem like you're trying to surround the harasser.

About two or three years ago I ran a house venue called Sour Haus, and we claimed "safer space," and I always felt good about it. It seemed to work fairly well. We did a number of things to protect the space and the people in it, we encouraged a sober space by making cookies and providing snacks and juices, we also hung signs, and I always had a backup team for situations in which someone had to be removed (it happened more than I thought it would). A lot of it was staying sober during shows, meeting each person, and keeping an eye out for any discomfort someone might be displaying. I

can understand that no matter how many safe space signs there were that it wasn't always easy to speak up, so I found it really important to check in with people.
—Rivanna Youngpool, booking agent for Gallery5

Check In

Taking one of the three action options doesn't mean your job is done, even if the creep is gone. The experience probably isn't over for the person you're trying to help. Trauma doesn't stop when the harassment is over or even when the harasser is out of sight.

So don't forget to follow up with the victim. If possible, just a quick "You still good? Okay, just let me know if anything else comes up" will suffice. If there was a big scene (like a harasser yelling loudly or being escorted out by security), it's helpful to address the crowd. They will be wondering what happened and if there's anything to worry about, and a quick public check-in will help. For example, "Sorry, everyone! Not sure what their problem was, but they're gone now. Please let any staff member know if you have any issues here—we don't tolerate harassment." This type of statement, just like your signage, is as much for potential victims as it is for potential harassers. And it goes a long way toward clearing the air if a considerate demeanor was used to get the offending person out (in order to prevent escalating the situation). After all, if a crowd thinks you were too friendly with an aggressor, they could understandably misinterpret your intentions and assume you are not taking the situation seriously. We'll talk more about "proactive" check-ins in the Take Initiative section later on.

Small Scenes

Every venue, scene, or milieu has its own challenges when it comes to making them safer. While you'll need to be flexible and ready to adapt your tactics, it's important to be mindful that most of the basics *don't* change. In other words, a particular situation might make you feel like a technique you've learned in this book isn't appropriate, but if you think about it and are honest with yourself, you might realize that you're prioritizing your needs or your fears over those of the victim. This can especially be true in small social scenes where most people know one another.

For instance, you might be wondering "What do I do if I know the person who is reporting harassment?" You respond in the *same exact way* you would if they were a stranger, regardless of your preexisting opinions. Believe the person reporting harassment, ground them if they are in crisis, validate their experience, offer them three basic options, and follow through. Your role is *not* to judge who is a good or bad person. Your role is simply to make your space free from harassment for however long you are present.

What if you know the person reported as the harasser? Well, that's different. Just kidding! There's nothing different about it. You still respond in the *same exact way*, up to and including asking them to leave. You can always chat more as a friend at another time, perhaps even discuss the incident, but while you are in your space, your role is to ensure the safety of all by upholding your safer spaces policy.

What if the people involved in the harassment know each other? Nothing excuses violent or sexually aggressive behavior—it doesn't matter if someone's partner was flirting with everyone at the bar. That doesn't justify abusive behavior. If one of them comes to you because they are scared, your job is to make them feel as safe as you can and make the situation as safe as you can.

Remember, you can always talk to fellow staff members if you have any questions or concerns about handling a complaint. You are a team!

Unless you're not. When the owner or manager is friends with a harasser, give them a chance to do right first. Speak to them privately about the situation while a coworker keeps an eye on the harasser. If the manager will not have the harasser kicked out, you can still let other patrons know you are not okay with that person's behavior by publicly telling them to stop—this lets everyone around you know that you, personally, do not approve and that you are doing *something*, which will validate the feelings of anyone who feels creeped out. It might also help you to not feel alone or crazy, since someone might approach you later and validate your feelings about that person's behavior or thank you for speaking up. You could also attempt to isolate the harasser and speak to them in private to temporarily get them away from the situation. Ask them to leave for the night, or have a conversation about how you're going to keep a close eye on them, cut them off from the bar, et cetera.

Illegal Spaces

Special provisions must be made for truly DIY spaces that have no legal protections or rights. Whether you've set up a cool vibe in the basement or living room of your house, or you're taking advantage of an abandoned or forgotten-about place, everyone who enters still has a right to feel as safe as possible. That includes all of the safer space tactics above (indications of who is responsible for the space, people who know grounding techniques, publicly posted anti-harassment policies, the works), plus a little more. Do what you can for fire safety: clear hallways, doorways, and windows of obstacles, clearly mark exits—even with spray paint, who cares? Have fire extinguishers on site and don't let bands or artists work with any flammable materials. It's not worth it. Don't risk your scene being outed by conservative trolls online; protect your identities in photos, don't post addresses on events or flyers ("Ask a punk" is not some cute saying, sometimes it's the only thing keeping your space from being discovered by people who want to take you down). Lastly, keep people healthy: have first-aid kits on hand, including EpiPens and Narcan. Lots of free water—whether people are coming down from drugs or are just really hot in a windowless basement, don't let anyone pass out. Just because the law doesn't know you exist doesn't mean you can't help validate the existence of everyone who walks through your doors.

Community connected me to the Bell Foundry. Queerness, transness, marginalization, outcast, these were all part of what brought folx here and precisely what made the space. No one was in charge, though there were responsibilities. It functioned as a dysfunctional collective.

I relocated there after my vaginoplasty, when a room opened up; as I had been a friend of the place for over a year. While this choice confused many of my friends, I valued the sanctuary. Sure other spaces were queer-affirming, but few of them backed that up with active establishment of the boundaries of their sanctuaries.

The Bell did.

Shows held in the basement led with taglines such as: "homophobia, transphobia, racism, sexism, and classism get the f*#k out!" And these statements were backed up by queers who took on the task of auditing offending individuals' participation in the space and also being accountable to sharing why such exclusion was happening. What I mean is: the organizers engaged in two-way accountability with the issues they were about instead of just talking about them.

In addition, the Bell was the only place in the warehouse queer scene where I had seen race diversity and class diversity actually in practice. There were upper-class queers, working-class queers, black, brown, and white folx all yelling about dishes and sharing herbs, sofas, and sounds. Too many intentional spaces are truly just white people in Baltimore.

As for safety, the technical issues of the stairway not being to fire code, and the electrical being exposed, were more than outweighed by the values of the community.

I would definitely risk infecting my neo-pussy again by moving in, had I to do it over.

I still laugh when I think about how the mayor gave me a medal for work in the trans community six months after evicting dozens of queer and trans folx from that building.

It was a place where no one looked.

And there was space to build.

—Ava Pipitone, executive director,
Baltimore Transgender Alliance

Take Initiative

You don't have to wait for an official complaint to deal with a situation. In fact, it's often better to address a problem before it escalates. Let's say you see a group of guys starting to surround a girl, or you see two people talking really intensely—maybe one is really uncomfortable and the other really angry. Feel free to eavesdrop! Make an assessment after watching for a moment, and take whatever action you feel is necessary. My friend Marty's golden rule for when he is unsure about whether or not to butt-in on a conversation: "I remind myself that this is my house and they're just a guest here!" You could wait until one person leaves to go to the bathroom or elsewhere and ask the uncomfortable person if they need anything. You can interrupt the conversation and share a little small talk, like asking them how they're doing or talking about the show or the music playing. It's your job to keep the peace, so what if you awkwardly talk to people in order to do so? By making your presence known early on, it shows everyone (harassers and targets alike) that you are aware of what happens in your space, identifying you as someone a victim can come to if needed and potentially preventing any further bad behavior.

Still feel awkward about approaching people? Ask for assistance from your coworkers. Either delegate to them entirely, or get them in on the routine. My bartender friend

Megan suggests that if a patron is doing something that is not permissible, you can ask another staff member or friend of the space to come in and *pretend* to do the same. You can then "warn them" or "kick them out," providing you with an example the actual problem person hopefully takes to heart. At the least it makes you look consistent when you kick them out. Striving to make life easier for folks can be complicated or take a little work, but once you get into the routine of looking out for others, it gets easier.

The Five D's of Bystander Intervention

Much of what I've said so far is based on the assumption that you're in charge of your space or at least in some position of official responsibility. That always helps, but you don't have to be on the payroll to have a positive effect on the situation. Even if you can't technically give the victim of harassment the same three options a manager might, you still have the power to stop violence and abuse. Basic bystander intervention skills can translate to many situations, and they are easy to share with others—the friends you're out clubbing with or coworkers in a space where the boss is a jerk who doesn't care about safety. You don't have to be confrontational toward harassers if you have your own safety concerns, just like you don't have to comfort victims if you fear coming across as cold or disingenuous. Learn the Five D's of Bystander Intervention listed below (developed by Hollaback! in partnership with the Green Dot Bystander Intervention Program), and see which ones work best for you. Then practice by role-playing some scenarios or taking a bystander intervention class in your area.

Direct

This is, well, the direct approach, in which you directly respond to harassment by naming what is happening or confronting the harasser. Be careful: this tactic can be risky. The harasser may redirect their abuse toward you and, that could escalate the situation. Before you decide to respond directly, assess the situation: Are you physically safe? Is the person being harassed physically safe? Does it seem unlikely that the situation will escalate? Can you tell if the person being harassed wants someone to speak up? If you can answer yes to all of these questions, you might choose a direct response.

Some things you can say to the harasser are:

- "That's inappropriate [disrespectful, not okay, etc.]"
- "Leave them alone."
- "That's homophobic [racist, etc.]"

The most important thing here is to keep it short and succinct. Try not to engage in dialogue, debate, or an argument, since this is how situations can escalate. If the harasser responds, try your best to assist the person who was targeted instead of engaging further with the harasser.

Again, use this one with caution.

Distract

Distraction is a subtler and more creative way to intervene. The aim here is simply to derail the incident by interrupting it. One way to do that is to ignore the harasser and engage directly with the person who is being targeted. Don't talk about or refer to the harassment. Instead, talk about something completely unrelated. If you feel comfortable, you might instead choose to engage with the harasser. Either way, you can try the following:

- Interrupt verbally. Pretend to be lost. Ask for the time. Pretend you know the person being harassed. Talk to them about something random and take attention off of the harasser.
- Get in the way physically and seemingly unintentionally. Continue what you were doing, but get between the harasser and the target.
- Accidentally-on-purpose spill your coffee or make a commotion.

Of course, you'll need to read the situation and choose your distraction method accordingly. The person who is being targeted will likely catch on. What they do in response can vary. Some harassers might slink away when they realize their behavior had witnesses. Others might get angry, but hopefully your act or statement will de-escalate the situation.

Delegate

Delegation is when you ask for assistance, for a resource, or for help from a third party. It can take various forms depending in the situation. The person you delegate to could be anyone from a store supervisor to a bus driver. If you're near a school, contact a teacher or someone at the front desk. On a college campus, contact campus security or someone at the front desk of a university building. Get your friend on board and have them use one of the methods of distraction to communicate with the person being harassed while you find someone else to delegate to.

Ultimately, the point is to speak to someone near you who notices—or is made to notice—what's happening and might be in a better position to intervene. Work together.

There's also the option of calling 311 or 911 to request help. Before contacting 911, use distraction to check in with the person being targeted to make sure they want you to do this. Some people may not be comfortable or safe with the intervention of law enforcement. For many, a history of being mistreated by law enforcement has led to justified fear and mistrust of police interventions. In our current social and political climate various communities, such as undocumented individuals, may feel less safe in the hands of police. Also, armed police officers have been known to escalate situations themselves. Just because calling the cops is a go-to response for some, it is not necessarily the best response in all situations. If you cannot reach the person in danger to ask if they want to call the police, you will need your use your best judgment.

Delayed

Even if you can't act in the moment, you can make a difference for the person who has been harassed by checking in on them after the fact. Many types of harassment happen in passing or very quickly. In such cases, you can wait until the situation is over and then speak to the person who was targeted. Here are some ways to use the delayed tactic:

- Ask if they're okay and tell them you're sorry that happened to them.
- Ask if there's any way you can support them.

63

- Offer to accompany them to their destination or to sit with them for awhile.
- Share resources and offer to help file a report if they want to.
- If you've documented the incident, ask if they want you to send it to them.

Document

And that brings us to documentation. It can be really helpful to record an incident as it is happening, but there are a number of things to keep in mind to safely and responsibly document harassment.[7]

First, assess the situation. Is anyone helping the person being harassed? If not, use one of the other four D's. If someone else is already helping out, assess your own safety. If you are safe, go ahead and start recording.

When doing so, make sure you keep a safe distance from the harasser. Film landmarks like street or subway platform signs and clearly state the date and time that you're filming. Keep the camera as stable as you can and film important shots for at least ten seconds. Most importantly, *always* ask the person who was harassed what they want to do with the recording. *Never* post it online or use it without their permission.

---

7   WITNESS, an organization that helps people use video and technology to defend human rights, has a great fact sheet called "Filming Hate" that discusses how to do so safely. It's available at https://witness.org/filming-hate.

You Are Powerful

Hopefully, by now you are getting the picture: everyone can do something. Hate crimes have been rising steadily in recent years. They increased by 12.5 percent in 2017, which was "the fourth consecutive annual rise in a row and the highest total in over a decade," according to the Center for the Study of Hate and Extremism.[8] So it is even more important that we show up for one another as active bystanders. People like you and me can make a difference—in fact, we're the only ones who will. Intervention, whether it's overhauling a space or helping a stranger on the street, isn't just the right thing to do, it also has a measurable effect. Research shows that even a knowing glance can significantly reduce trauma for the person who is targeted. One of the most important things we can do is to let them know, in some way, however big or small, that they are not alone.

Okay, I'm Powerful, but What Do I Do?

We all have many roles as we move through the spaces we use and inhabit. Being "in charge" of a space, as we've seen, isn't the only role that can respond to harassment. Between a relatively uninvolved bystander and a hopefully invested, engaged manager or collective, there are often a number of intermediate roles. In the music world—and I think that, with minor adjustments, this can apply to most environments—two main roles that people take on, that don't

---

8   Center for the Study of Hate and Extremism, *Hate Crimes Rise in U.S. Cities and Counties in Time of Division and Foreign Interference* (San Bernadino: California State University, 2018), 3.

involve literally running the place, are *artist* and *audience*. Let's take a look at each.

Artist

Whether you have a microphone in front of you or your newest painting is hanging on the wall behind you, you have a platform. People are gathered for you. You don't want anyone to leave because some jerk is ruining their good time, right?

No matter what the gallery or club's policies are, people will listen when you announce yours. That attention begins even before you enter the space. Let people know what you stand for (and what you won't stand for) by making it clear in everything you do. Make social media posts supporting organizations that address social justice issues. For specific events, include language on the flyer or event page that "harassment is not okay at our show" or that "no sexist, racist, homophobic, or xenophobic bullshit will be tolerated." Most importantly, personalize it—you know your audience! You know how to speak to them in a way that will resonate. Hell, if they are fans, you've already been talking to them for a while.

The night of your gig or opening, make a speech or mention between songs that if anyone is harassed they can come talk to you. You also have a relationship with the venue that the audience does not have. Get on the same page with them before the night gets hectic. Ask to whom you should refer incidents of harassment if they occur, making it easier for you to *delegate* if you are too busy to help someone appropriately.

If the venue doesn't have a policy or doesn't understand the importance of one, ask them why not. Preach. Tell them it's important to you and other artists you know that your audience feels safe and welcome at your shows. You might be surprised by how receptive they are.

Have a lot of clout? That means you can *demand* that the venues you work with adopt the policies contained in this book before you will perform there again.

If you really want to get DIY with it, *make* the venue a safer space the night you're there. Put up your own trans-friendly signs, put homemade bystander information cards everywhere, invite a local nonprofit that deals with racial injustice or gender-based violence to table next to you, bring an "official listener" or "peer listener" with you (someone who is trained in grounding techniques and can hand out resources if people need them during the night). Finally, if you're like me, you travel with a band or crew or have one back home handling aspects of your business. Get your manager, bandmates, and merch person up to speed on active listening and crisis response. Bystander intervention is a team effort. It will lessen the burden on you if you're not the only one who knows these skills, and it makes it easier for victims to find support at your events.

Speedy Ortiz: A Case Study

The American rock band Speedy Ortiz is a great example of using the power you have and inspiring others to join you when you do. Back in 2015, they set up an anonymous text hotline (via Google Voice) that allowed audience members to chat with a designated person (sometimes a band member or crew, sometimes a point person for the club—decided the night of the show) about what kind of help they need. So if someone overheard transphobic language, for instance, and was stuck in the middle of a large festival crowd and couldn't see who to tell, or wanted someone to walk them to their car, but either didn't know who to talk to at the venue or didn't trust they'd be believed, then the band and their crew could act as the facilitator between the venue and the audience member. In their contract rider for shows (where the kind of beer you prefer normally goes), they include a section asking for venues to be, in essence, a safer space for the night. They request safer space signage at their shows (or put it up themselves), basically saying, as Sadie Dupuis, the lead singer and guitarist, told me, "We do not tolerate harassment or bigoted language at our shows. Be considerate of other people, don't touch anyone without their consent, really basic, basic stuff, along with the text number to contact if there's any problem." They hand out postcards with the Five D's of Bystander Intervention and make sure someone on the tour knows grounding techniques. In the fall of 2018, they took donations from music sales on their Bandcamp page to cover the costs of handing out copies of my pocket guide to all the venues they played while on tour with Liz Phair. Be still my beating heart! Other bands have taken note too. When Speedy Ortiz toured with Against Me!, Sadie said they loved the ideas and were eager to help. Modern Baseball also set up their own hotline, and for larger venues and festivals they put the phone number really big on the screen behind them so everyone can see.

Sadie also told me,

> It's a conversation every time we advance a show. Sometimes I'll send over a rider, and they'll say, 'Hey, this is great. Here's our safer spaces policy—do you want this in addition to yours, or...?' and I'll be like, 'No, actually, yours is better.' Or I'll ask for gender-neutral bathrooms, and they'll be, like, 'Oh, okay, our signs say urinals and stalls, do you want something different?' And I can say 'No, you already did the thing,' which is great. And there have also been venues that have said, 'We don't have anything like this, I love this idea, how can we help?' and their whole staff will meet up before the show and talk about some of the stuff.
>
> The more bands and artists take safer spaces into their own hands, the more audiences will begin to expect it, and the more venues will have to take notice.

Audience

An audience is more than just a collection of unrelated bystanders. You are all sharing an experience. You are united by a common reason for coming together in a particular space. You're a community, and, as in any community, there is power in numbers.

Whether they want to admit it or not, both artists and venues rely on you, the audience, to keep the wheels turning. Without you, nothing happens. That's why one common tactic audiences have used is the boycott. You've read about them, maybe even participated in them, I'm sure. With a boycott, audiences pressure venues or performers by removing their support (and their dollars) until an identified behavior or policy is changed. The boycott is a tried-and-true method of protest.

That's cool. I'm all for them, but I'd like to focus on what you can *do* rather than what you can temporarily stop doing. After all, if our goal is a less violent world, focusing on the positive change you can make locally is a perfect place to start. Left to their own devices, people and spaces causing harm will just continue to do so, whether you run them out of town or not. Those of us in the audience—and, by that, I mean those of us who are *not* directly in harm's way at that particular time—should consider calmly and directly letting venues and artists know that the behavior they are engaging in is harmful and what they can do instead. It's not for us to decide how a victim should respond to their harm or abuse, but as an outsider we're better able to change minds when we come from a place of love, no judgment, and a true desire to make things better.

To be clear, I believe in diverse tactics because we are diverse people. Sometimes it does take a figurative hit on the head to realize you've made a mistake and need to do better. But I am not concerned whether we have enough people out there who will hit these folks on the head. I'm asking for an equal or greater number of people—not victims—to take the time to talk with, and educate those around them. Yeah, it takes work and it isn't always fair, and you don't always have to be the one to do it, but if not you, then who?

How about some other, easier things you can do? Submit information about a venue to Is This Venue Accessible?, a website that helps people with mobility issues plan their nights out. Submit a public restroom that is safe for transgender, intersex, and gender-nonconforming individuals on the REFUGE Restrooms app or website.[9] Intervene every time you see something off. Stand up to your friends when they make offensive or derogatory remarks. It doesn't have to be a full-on, organized boycott, but don't pay for music made by racist, sexist, or transphobic people, and prioritize paying for and supporting media made by folks who aren't white men. Be a buddy for your friend who thinks a punk show is too scary or aggro for them, and stand with them all night so they can still attend. Share this book with friends, and buy a copy for your favorite venue or, better yet, all your local venues. You can also buy multiple copies of this book or the pocket guide version at a discount and sell them at whatever functions you table at.

While this goes against the grain of a society that tells us we should wait around for this or that authority to fix things for us, the point is to recognize what power you do have, and then use it. Even if you prevent one person from having to experience harassment, for one moment, it's worth it. Championing a cause in front of thousands of people is great,

---

9   Is This Venue Accessible? can be found at http://itvaccessible.com and REFUGE Restrooms is at https://www.refugerestrooms.org.

and more artists should do it, but you have the potential to make an even bigger impact on individual lives by doing what you can during those small, easy-to-ignore moments. Don't ignore them anymore.

The Influence of Alcohol: For Bartenders (and Anyone Else Paying Attention)

Many of us, even the most "woke" or feminist, can fall victim to a subtle bias when it comes to alcohol. If someone gets drunk, the dubious logic goes, isn't it partially their fault if someone takes advantage of them?

No. It isn't. Whether someone is drunk, drugged, or over-served, everyone still deserves to get home safe. Bartenders are in a good position to see the signs, but anyone can keep an eye out. Here are some things to keep in mind if your space encounters an inebriated person who is likely to become a target of assault or violence or to be the person engaging in it.

Men are more likely to be aggressive or commit assault when drinking.[10] This doesn't let abusers off the hook. Abusive behavior is unacceptable, period. Instead of faulting drug or alcohol use itself, we need to make it clear that it is no excuse to harass or assault anyone.

So if you have a good tactic for cutting people off from alcohol without them making a scene about it, share it with your coworkers. You might say: "You know what? You're

---

10 See K. D. Scott, J. Schafer, and T. K. Greenfield, "The Roles of Alcohol in Physical Assault Perpetration and Victimization," *Journal of Studies on Alcohol and Drugs* (1999): 528–536.

feeling great, but your hand is empty. Let me get you some sparkling water—you want a lime or lemon in it?" Giving them a choice makes them feel in control, lessening the chances of them getting angry at a bartender telling them what to do. Similarly, "How about I get you some water for now, and you can come see me again when you finish it?" could work, especially if you give them a *big* cup of water. You can also simply ignore the requests of anyone who is drinking far too much and just not respond at all. The bartender wields the power because the bartender distributes the drinks! So use your power for good.

Then there are the dudes who seem to be trying to get other people drunk and thereby creating more potential targets. This could just be some overeager party animal, but it could also be a red flag. If you think someone is acting suspiciously, try to remember their names when you swipe their credit card or check their IDs. There are also some common behaviors that predators engage in that you can be aware of. For instance, look out for someone who makes the rounds and talks to every customer in the bar but isn't friends with them. They could be cruising for a vulnerable target—and are also probably creeping people out. Also take note of anyone buying rounds of shots for a large group and trying to hand them out themself. Make each person come to the bar to drink their individual shot. This can help you keep eyes on everyone's behavior before and after taking the shot. If it doesn't prevent any predatory tampering with drinks, it will help you assess if anyone has been roofied.

Potential victims are vulnerable when drunk, whether they got that way themselves or had some ill-intentioned help. Some of the signs that the latter may have happened are:

- They went from sober to drunk very quickly.
- They have trouble controlling their movements or have slurred speech.
- They have dizziness, blurred vision, confusion, or nausea.
- Someone they haven't interacted with all night now wants to take them home.

So what should you do? Stay with the victim, get them water, call their friend, take them to a hospital (if they are at risk of accidental overdose), whatever you have to do. The person who spiked their drink could still be targeting them, so it's important they make it to a safe and secure location.

If you're in a position to do so, and if it doesn't violate your community's standards, consider installing security cameras. Whether the victim wants to pursue legal action or not (and you should take your cues from the victim), you can at least ban this person from your establishment. Legally, touching someone without their consent, when that touching is sexual, is sexual assault and a criminal offense. Being able to give consent means you have the freedom and capacity to make your choices. If someone is drunk or on drugs, they cannot legally give consent. But, legality aside, anyone drugging or groping people shouldn't be welcome in your, or any, space.

There is a private Facebook group for bartenders and bar staff in Baltimore to communicate about people who pose a safety risk. They share information and photos or descriptions of patrons who are difficult (aggressive or disrespectful) or have been banned for harassment or violence. Networks like these are a form of safety planning, and they allow people to warn each other about potentially harmful behavior. Of course, it's good to keep in mind that nothing on the internet is fully private, so unless you witnessed behavior firsthand, it's better to use "alleged" when appropriate.

I started volunteering at Bridgetown DIY around 2.5 years ago. It is one of few all ages, DIY spaces in the L.A. area that hosts bands/workshops/programs that offers an alternative to a 21+ bar focused on alcohol sales.

Although people are allowed to drink prior to visiting the space, we don't allow drinking inside or directly outside the space. In order to implement that rule, we explain our safer space policy and ask people to please drink away from the space if they absolutely have to. That has sometimes resulted in anger and retaliation, and we are then forced to make people leave the space.

I have personally witnessed a fight during a show, which moved to the parking lot. I felt scared and fully aware of my inability to really do anything because of my small stature. Another volunteer came to back me up, and we asked the person who booked the show to make an announcement before the next set about our safer space policy and that violence of any kind would not be tolerated.

Ideally, we hope that engaging with people in a calm manner will educate them about the value of safer spaces, but sometimes people can't be reasoned with and we hope they choose not to come back to the space. We also make sure to vet bands (browse their social media, ask around about them) to find out if they will follow our policies. We also have a safer space mission statement on our Facebook page and posted around the space.

—Erica Shultz, core volunteer and keyholder,
Bridgetown DIY

Larger Spaces

I've seen firsthand how difficult it is to coordinate public safety at a large gathering, like a festival or concert with thousands of people in attendance. You have to consider weather (staying alert and up to speed on current conditions, as in lightning, tornadoes, hurricanes, having clear storm shelter locations, etc.), fire safety (pathways, exits, inflammable materials), emergency services (EMTs on site, free water and shade, first aid supplies, defibrillators), and even mass shootings (trained security staff, pat-downs or metal-detecting wands), while ensuring you are following the local laws and protocols. The sheer number of people statistically increases the chances of *something* happening, and that absolutely includes harassment or violence.

Kari Sampsel, an emergency room doctor and director of the Ottawa Hospital Sexual Assault and Partner Abuse Care Program, conducted a study that looked at the extremely high rates of sexual violence occurring at large events. Her research showed that approximately 25 percent of the sexual assault cases her organization saw in 2013 occurred at large events. Out of these cases, the majority tended to be young women, and less than one-third knew the person who had assaulted them.[11]

While it is unreasonable to hold the coordinators of large gatherings personally responsible for individual incidents of violence against women or people of color, I believe more can be done to prevent and prepare for these incidents than is currently standard in the music industry. Street harassment (harassment in public spaces from strangers) is a public health issue. If you are prepared and have public policies for what to do if there is a fire, what audiences are allowed to bring into a venue, or where to go if you hit your head in the mosh pit, there's no reason not to also have them for harassment and violence.

Whether we are talking about large or small gatherings, most of the same points I've touched on apply. Have obvious signage: on your website, all around the venue, in every bathroom, and in every info packet. Train security and other staff to believe, listen to, and validate victims' concerns. You might already have protocol in place for which form to fill out or who to report each incident to, but if your staff is dismissive of a victim in the moments after harassment has happened, they are making things worse. If you want security to concentrate on preventing stage-diving or the sneaking in of alcohol or weapons, that's fine. Just make it clear where people can to go to report incidents when they occur, and ensure someone is there and trained to deal with it when it does.

---

11 Zoë Argiropulos-Hunter, "How Local Voices Are Changing the Conversation about Sexual Assault at Music Festivals," *Ottawa Beat*, August 2017.

Many festivals use local hires for security who are trained by their own company, not the festival itself. Depending on the size of the event, I realize I might be asking you to train over a hundred people to be more victim-centered for one day of work. This comes down to using the power you already have. You are about to spend lots of money with one company to provide you with security, so it is absolutely reasonable to ask everyone to respond to a victim in a supportive way. Post signs in all the break areas. Email information in advance, and ask they share it with all their workers. Sure, it's another thing to think about, but it's one or two extra steps at most. You can do it.

And you don't have to do it alone. There are groups out there currently doing the work of raising awareness about harassment at music festivals, helping to craft festival policies, training staff, musicians, and audience members, hosting discussions, creating surveys, and in general sharing their expertise to help make *everyone's* show-going experience more fun. For a big production, you don't hire a head of security who's never done security before, and you especially don't let your random cousin volunteer to do it thinking "how hard can it be?" No, you get an expert. So hire an expert, a consultant, to ensure you're doing as much for your audience as possible to keep them safe from harassment, rape, and assault. Some organizations currently active include OurMusicMyBody, Project Soundcheck, Safe Gigs for Women, Good Night Out, and A Voice for the Innocent, as well as individuals like me.

I'm really excited about organizations like the Canadian Independent Music Community and Calling All Crows (USA) who are using their larger platforms to influence large and small venues alike. CIMC held an "Anti-Harassment

Summit" in early 2018 to discuss finding industry-wide solutions to all forms of harassment. Their objectives included:

1. Implementation of a Code of Conduct that can be adhered to, or used as an example, by large and small music performance venues/festivals, recording studios, music companies and the many varying workplaces in the music community.
2. Set standards that will protect: a. artists, musicians, technical staff, administrative staff and audience; b. whether they are clients, volunteers, employees, dependent contractors or independent contractors, board directors; and c. regardless of their representation by an association, guild or union, or not represented at all.
3. Recognition that there must be zero tolerance for all forms of harassment in the music community.
4. Creation of education and prevention resources and tools that will help the music community address claims and complaints.
5. Seek ways to provide resources and support in cases of harassment, and how to seek support.[12]

Of course, with bigger initiatives, there is always the risk that there will be no real impact, that it's just for show. I'm hopeful that if we can get larger venues and festivals (i.e., the

---

12 "Canadian Music Community Anti-Harassment Summit," Canadian Independent Music Community, April 24, 2018, https://cimamusic.ca/news/recent-news/read,article/17610/canadian-music-community-anti-harassment-summit.

moneymakers) to pay attention, preventing and addressing harassment could become an industry standard. Anything that makes it easier for people to talk about it, whether they are experiencing it or in charge of addressing it, is worth it.

It's About Them, Not You

Every instance of harassment is a little unique, and maybe there are no perfect responses, but there are lots of possible responses. It's largely a matter of realizing that fact and committing those possibilities to memory. Thanks to the tireless efforts of women's rights movements, sexual assault advocates, and civil rights movements, people have figured out which ones work, and anyone (with some time and effort) can train themselves to "naturally" do the right thing when the situation calls for it. Leaving things up to chance means letting the most common cultural biases take over. We don't want that, because those biases and inequalities created the problem in the first place. Don't leave other people's safety and well-being to chance. Learn the tactics, share your skills with others, center the victim, and interrupt violence and harassment every single time you see it.

three

ACCOUNTABILITY

You WILL MAKE mistakes. We all do. It's how you handle them that matters.

Your mistakes will likely fall into two categories: things you've done and things you've failed to do. And those, in turn, might be wrongs committed by you personally, by someone else in your space, or by the space and its policies (problems of planning and/or follow-through).

Maybe it was a personal slipup; you misspoke, misunderstood what was going on, or didn't know that what you said is considered offensive. Or maybe you contributed to an unsafe environment for a group of people and only later understood your role in it and how harmful it was to others.

Or maybe you don't care about the altruistic reasons to make your business safer, and you're only reading this because you don't want to see a drop in attendance or get slapped with a lawsuit. Hey, I'm not judging (much): a safer place is a safer place.

There are many reasons to want to change for the better, but the time when a business could be silent and wait for an incident to blow over is gone. Whatever the situation, the basics of a healthy response are simple: you must acknowledge what happened, apologize for your role in it, and make amends.

Was your mistake accidental and fairly minor? Immediately apologize, and do so sincerely. You can explain that it wasn't what you meant to say, that you know better, or that you didn't know that word was offensive. This is not meant to excuse your behavior; it is only a segue to explain precisely what you'll do differently from now on. Just as memorizing certain phrases and ideas helps you in the moment of dealing with harassment, learning a few helpful phrases like "It won't happen again," "I'll do better next time," and "Thanks for pointing that out, I wouldn't want to offend anyone else" can aid you in your apology. Of course, this isn't just rote memorization, and you're not learning these sentences as a way of deflecting criticism. You have to mean them.

Finally, if everyone is moving on to the next topic, let them. Otherwise you risk making this moment about you, and it's not.

What if it's a bigger incident, one in which more people deserve an explanation? Let's say you found out that one of your security guards has been touching female patrons inappropriately. You don't know how many people have been affected by this, because many women might not have come forward, not trusting your venue to handle something like this correctly after having their trust (and bodies) violated. This situation would call for a public apology, preferably one that provides an easy way for people to report new complaints. The public apology should come after you've reached out to all the known individuals affected by this employee's actions. Let's break the apology down to figure out how it should—and shouldn't—work.

How to Apologize

It should be straightforward, right? You just sincerely apologize for what you did (or for your part in what happened), and that's that. Not exactly.

Language matters. It can highlight subtle biases in how you are seeing and understanding the situation. People, especially those most affected by violence and harassment, will pick up on those quickly—not even necessarily consciously. For instance, do not say "if I offended you," or "I'm sorry you feel that way." Framing things that way implies that you are apologizing for *their* feelings, when you should be apologizing for *your* behavior, actions, or inaction, depending on the situation.

Saying the right things in the right way isn't like studying for a test and spewing the correct answers. Being careful and intentional with your language helps you *think* carefully and intentionally, to mean what you say, to understand what's going on, what people need from you, as well as all the "outs" and wiggle room that patriarchal culture offers people in (relative) power to not really take responsibility for, let alone make amends for, the harm they've caused marginalized people.

So state clearly what you should have done instead and/or how you will change things in the future to ensure it does not happen again. In the situation described above, firing that security guard and any others who knew about his actions (but did or said nothing) would be a good first step. After that, you should, at the very least, want to hire new security staff, some of whom are not cisgender men, and give them all training in how to appropriately interact with customers. Given that every space is different, you could ask for suggestions from your patrons, though this is not a way to get others to do your work for you. You need to do the research, find the resources, and understand how it all applies to your venue. Moving forward, you should provide an anonymous way for people to submit complaints of harassment in your establishment (whether by your staff or other patrons), ensuring that they experience no negative consequences when they do.

Speaking of communication, this is yet another time that active listening skills come in handy. Giving victims your full attention, really hearing them, and letting them know that you've heard them will make things go much more smoothly. Active listening helps you drop the sorts of self-serving defenses that prevent you from seeing things clearly and thus, from fixing actual problems rather than what you imagine (or wish) those problems to be.

If you run a business and are hearing about an incident in real time from a victim, in addition to your apologies and actions to make the situation right, you can offer to make it up to them directly with free admission to the next show, a free drink or meal, or whatever goods or services you can give. Understand that they might refuse, especially if your offer could be read as promotion for your business, along the lines of "Here's a free shirt with our name on it!" It's important to let them know that you are willing to do what you can in order to regain their trust.

In a 2018 study, where the researchers were able to directly analyze video footage of customer service desk interactions at two busy airports, two broad conclusions were drawn.[1] The first was that "customers cared less about the actual outcome than about the process by which the employee tried to offer assistance." For our purposes, that roughly translates to the fact that victims are not holding you personally responsible for the harassment they have endured from someone else, but they will hold you responsible for how you handle their complaint. The second broad conclusion? Being overly apologetic does little to satisfy a dissatisfied customer. To be frank, it can be read as weak and passive when people are looking for an active attitude of responsibility and reparations. But someone who uses active listening to ensure they understand the grievance, sincerely apologizes, and then moves swiftly to rectify the situation is seen as capable, putting others at ease more quickly. "Sorry" is not usually enough, and empty repetitions only make matters worse. You must take action.

It's also good form to create and post public policies that specifically address how the incident could have been prevented or handled better. If you already had policies in place, and they failed you, update them. Consult local experts,

---

1   Detelina Marinova, Sunil K. Singh, and Jagdip Singh, "Frontline Problem-Solving Effectiveness: A Dynamic Analysis of Verbal and Nonverbal Cues," *Journal of Marketing Research* 55, no. 2 (April 2018): 178–192.

search the internet. The more prep work you do, the easier it is to handle these situations when they occur.

Recognize that the individuals involved might not ever forgive you. Just because you have apologized does not mean you are entitled to forgiveness—that's not the goal of an apology! You can't predict or control a victim's reaction. Going back to "how things used to be, like it never even happened," is not the goal of this process. Whether they think you really messed up, or don't feel relaxed there anymore, or your space (or face) just makes them think of what happened to them, they might not want to return ever again. All of those reasons are valid, and none of them mean you apologized "for nothing." If you have truly made efforts to ensure that a similar incident won't happen again (and, if relevant, the community has been notified of these changes), then you have not only helped people process the hurt they've put up with, but you also will help prevent future hurts. You don't want to go back to the way things were anyway—you know more now, you're wiser, more empathic, kinder.

Sometimes people who were not there or don't know the entire story will bring up old incidents. While frustrating, it's a waste of energy to remain angry or annoyed by them. Instead, focus on the positive. Continue to improve as a safer space because it's the right thing to do, not for recognition or accolades.

Okay, next step. There are bad apologies and good apologies. Learn the difference!

A bad apology changes the subject. It minimizes what happened and, therefore, the blame based on what happened. A bad apology took too long to issue and does not mention the victim(s) or what you did or let happen to them. It is often just a pivot to a "comeback." A bad apology is about how you made people feel instead of what you did—or, even worse, it's all about how you feel.

Let's look at some examples:

After being accused of harassment and violent abuse by twenty different women, Jian Ghomeshi (a Canadian musician and radio personality) wrote an essay in 2018 for the *New York Review of Books*. It read, in part: "What I do confess is that I was emotionally thoughtless in the way I treated those I dated and tried to date."[2] This is clearly sleight-of-hand. He was not accused of "thoughtlessness" but of punching, biting, and otherwise harming women. By only admitting (potentially on the advice of a lawyer) to something that most people could identify with (being thoughtless from time to time), he did not actually take responsibility. He was only demonstrating that he still did not understand, or was unwilling to admit, the severity of his actions, while lamenting the fact that he had suffered "enough humiliation for a lifetime."[3]

Then there was the 2017 Dove advertisement that was criticized for being racist. Specifics of the ad aside, the company's customer base was upset. In response, Dove tweeted: "An image we recently posted on Facebook missed the mark in representing women of color thoughtfully. We deeply regret the offense it caused."[4] This is not a great response. They

---

2   Jian Ghomeshi, "Reflections of a Hashtag," *New York Review of Books* 65, no. 15 (October 11, 2018), https://www.nybooks.com/articles/2018/10/11/reflections-hashtag/.

3   Ibid.

4   Katie Richards, "Dove Apologizes for Posting Racially Insensitive Ad

displaced blame by saying "the image" missed the mark, not them. Not to mention that what they were accused of was racism, not "missing the mark." Also, they did not use the words "sorry" or "apologize" anywhere. Rather, they regret the "offense"—in other words they regret the feelings of those they offended.

Okay, let's try an extreme example. After a massive rig explosion and oil spill in the Gulf of Mexico in 2010, BP's then-CEO, Tony Hayward, started out strong in a news interview, stating, "The first thing to say [to the people of Louisiana] is 'I'm sorry.'" He then went on to add, "We're sorry for the massive disruption it has caused their lives. There's no one who wants this over more than I do. I would like my life back." Now, keep in mind, this was said in regard to a rig explosion that killed eleven workers. It's difficult to set the tragedy of the situation aside—or the fact that a giant corporation will always be serving its own interests, and brand, when it apologizes—but let's just try to focus on his bad apology and how we can learn from his egregious mistake.

Your apologies should not try to equate *any* of your suffering with the suffering you have caused (or helped to cause) others. If you are coming from an emotional or defensive place, it might not be the best time for you to make a big, thorough apology. Give people something, keep it simple, and make a promise to come back to it later (and keep your word). You will only make things worse by prioritizing yourself and your feelings, by speaking without thinking, or by

---

on Facebook That 'Missed the Mark,'" *Adweek*, October 8, 2017, https://www.adweek.com/brand-marketing/dove-apologizes-for-posting-racially-insensitive-ad-on-facebook-that-missed-the-mark.

not communicating that a full statement is forthcoming (once you calm down).

Everyone has a right to their feelings, but it's best to use the Ring Theory to determine with whom you should share those feelings. Created by Susan Silk after a bout with breast cancer, the Ring Theory is a simple exercise to help you avoid saying the wrong thing in a bad situation. Here's how it works:

> Draw a circle. This is the center ring. In it, put the name of the person at the center of the current trauma…. Now draw a larger circle around the first one. In that ring put the name of the person next closest to the trauma…. Repeat the process as many times as you need to. In each larger ring put the next closest people. Parents and children before more distant relatives. Intimate friends in smaller rings, less intimate friends in larger ones. When you are done you have a Kvetching Order…. Here are the rules. The person in the center ring can say anything she wants to anyone, anywhere. She can kvetch and complain and whine and moan and curse the heavens and say, "Life is unfair" and "Why me?" That's the one payoff for being in the center ring.[5]

---

5   Susan Silk and Barry Goldman, "How Not to Say the Wrong Thing," *Los Angeles Times*, April 7, 2013, http://articles.latimes.com/2013/ apr/07/opinion/la-oe-0407-silk-ring-theory-20130407.

And the people in other circles? They can complain and focus on their feelings, but only to people in circles further out than theirs. Support and comfort move inward, dumping your own feelings moves outward.

So, yes, Tony Hayward may have been really stressed out dealing with a company crisis, but by saying so much publicly and letting it get back to the families of the workers who died, he was dumping on the rings more inward than his, when he should have turned outward to his wife or close friends. There are appropriate ways to express feelings that don't make the situations worse, and sometimes your feelings have no place in an apology you're giving.

A good apology is from the heart. It puts the victims first and uses the words "I am sorry." It demonstrates remorse and empathy, addressing and clearly stating what you did that caused harm. A good apology is also timely but not rushed. It should show a commitment to grow and change. When making it, you should give options for appropriate recompense. Finally, a good apology is not a marketing strategy.

One of my favorite, if fanciful, examples of a good apology is the one that author Lauren Hough imagined in a tweet she posted: "You know what would be fucking weird to hear? 'I did that. It was fucking terrible. I am sorry. I did years of therapy and soul searching and work and I changed my behavior. I can't change what I did, but I made damn sure I never did it again.' Why is that never the statement?"[6]

My friend Jacq Jones, sex educator and owner of Sugar, was kind enough to share her experience making a public apology:

---

6   Lauren Hough (@laurenthehough), Twitter.com, September 17, 2018.

We were one of the first places to receive safer space training from Hollaback! Sugar is an education-focused, sex-positive sex toy store. We've worked hard to be a safer space since we opened our doors in 2007. Our staff is trained from the day they start that certain behaviors are not tolerated within our walls, and staff has the full support of management in requiring a customer who is overstepping boundaries to leave our space. We encourage staff to first attempt to de-escalate situations and model appropriate behavior and speech. That works 99% of the time. But occasionally, someone just doesn't get it and can't be in the store. We do that for the safety of our customers, our staff, and our brand.

One of the most valuable aspects of the safer space training was the manual. Since the training, almost all of the staff (other than me) has turned over. But every staff member since has been required to review the manual on their first or second day on the job.

Recently it came out that a nationally known educator, who has taught at the store on multiple occasions, violated someone's consent. I was horrified. And also not shocked. Humans make mistakes. But then his response was not good. In fact it was bad. It quickly became clear that he had violated other people's boundaries on multiple occasions. I had to spend some time thinking about how Sugar needed to respond. And in where our responsibilities, and my own responsibility, lay. The truth is, I had seen this person push people's boundaries. And simply written it off as him "being a guy." I never spoke to him about his actions. I assumed that he was simply a little pushy sometimes, a little over-enthusiastic, and that it stopped there. That was a bad assumption. It's one I won't make again.

So. I had fucked up and exposed my staff and my customers to someone who may have caused them harm. I cried. I talked to friends. I talked to my brother.

I wrote a blog post about what had happened and my own poor judgment.[7] I offered a route to a transformative justice process for anyone that had been harmed by my actions. The post went up on all of our social media platforms, but first I sent it to the educator. He is someone that I care about. Whom I've known for over a decade. One of my core beliefs is that people can grow and change. That people (and businesses are just organizations run by people) will inevitably fuck up. When we do, we must, even when it's painful, look for our responsibility and for ways to promote healing. And we have to use that to shift our

---

7   Jacq Jones, "Consent, Reid Mihalko and Accountability," Sugar, http://www.sugartheshop.com/blogs/sugar-blog/consent-reid-mihalko-and-accountability.

actions going forward. And make our spaces a little bit safer.

I also personally love the succinct way that activist and educator Rania El Mugammar breaks down the elements of a good apology. For her, it means acknowledging and then centering the hurt we have caused. "It's not about our feelings of guilt, but about the feelings and needs of those we have harmed. Those we've harmed shouldn't have to support us during an apology, nor should they have to coach or cheer for us."[8] At the same time, she says that we must let go or "divest from" our need for forgiveness: "Invest in the labor of reconciliation, divorced from appeasing our feelings of guilt and focusing on healing and supporting those we've harmed. Apologize without forgiveness as a target, but healing, regardless of whether we're forgiven or not."

Interpersonal Relationships

These lessons are not simply to be used in crisis situations; they're not behind some pane of glass that's to be broken in case of emergency. In fact, a measure of how well you've learned them is the degree to which you take them home with you and into your personal lives. It's a lot easier to be the better person in public when you are part of the team of good guys fighting evil in this world. In certain circles—more and more of them these days—*not* learning how to apologize, improve, and make amends simply won't be tolerated.

---

8 Rania El Mugammar, "Anatomy of an Apology," Rania Writes, http://www.raniawrites.com/anatomyofanapology.html.

Use your active listening skills in everyday life. Your partner doesn't want to hear "You know what you should do?" when they complain about their boss. They want you to listen! So take a moment, stop scrolling on your phone, look them in the eye and commiserate with them. When I'm not sure what my bestie expects of me when she talks about a problem she's having, and then there's that pause—"Oh jeez, is it my turn? What am I supposed to say?!"— I find it helpful to be blunt and ask "What kind of listener do you need right now? Do you just need to vent? Wanna hear what I would do or what I've done in similar situations? Either way, I'm here for you—this *does* sound like a totally frustrating, maddening, disheartening situation."

Apologize like a champ and learn from your mistakes. This is a really tough one for me. I'm very good at rushing through those tough conversations with people I've hurt to avoid sitting with the discomfort. But by avoiding it for so long, once I did make strides to be better, the idea that I hurt someone seemed way heavier than it should have. I would feel so bad that my apologies became about me and my feelings. I am still learning that messing up has no direct correlation to your worth as a person. One way to do that is understanding that how you respond when you make a mistake will either make the situation better or worse.

Let's walk through how an apology for a common, small mistake might look.

Keep the focus on the person you're apologizing to. Let them say their piece, really hear them, then tell them why you're sorry: "I'm so sorry I forgot to load the dishwasher. I know how frustrating that is for you because you expected

94

to come home late after a long day of work and be able to prepare your dinner without a big mess in your way." Then address what they said ("I know you asked me if I had time to do it, and I said I would") before you make it about you ("but this meeting with the West Coast chapter went long, and I just couldn't get away"). Then offer a solution or recompense: "But I'm happy to clear some space for you now, or I can even reheat my leftovers for you. Or do you want me to order a pizza? How can I make it up to you?"

Hopefully they see the sincerity in your desire to make it right. Following through with something you agreed to do and wanting to do right by your partner is a much better approach than "I'm sorry! I was in a meeting! Jeez!" That helps no one. Also, learn from your mistakes! In the above example, maybe that means not promising to do the dishes when you know your meetings normally run late, or maybe it means doing them before the meeting starts. If your partner stays a little hangry until they get a chance to eat, let them feel their feelings without getting angry yourself—you gave an appropriate (and good) apology for your mistake, and it's natural that you would be ready to move on before them.

Talk to a pro. If you haven't already, consider talking with a counselor to work on shedding some of the bad communication habits and coping skills you've picked up over time. We all have them! How do you think I got better at not falling apart every time I upset someone? Certainly not on my own. I needed a professional to hold a mirror up to my faults because mine was, well, faulty. When therapy is cost prohibitive, you have to guide yourself through the work. I've left a list of books in the appendix to help get you started.

We can't let our coping mechanisms for this unjust world turn into the abuse of others. Learning to avoid confrontation altogether is not healthy. Neither is acting out or being aggressive. These behaviors might have helped you survive growing up—whether they were the only way to be seen or to avoid being seen—but they're not doing you any favors now that you have grown up. Don't put your shit on others. They have their own; they shouldn't have to take on yours too. It's easy to forget that most of the influential interactions we have are on the individual level. Whether we want to become the best partners, friends, family members, or allies, we must heal ourselves first. Bring the best version of yourself to the fight.

> We all mess up, but most of the time people want you to recover when you stumble. I sometimes think that maybe half of performance is teetering on the edge of completely falling apart on stage in front of everyone, but never quite letting it happen. When we screw up, I think the best way to roll out of it is to own that it happened. Apologize if you need to. Welcome the humiliation, and do better next time.
>
> —Rahne Alexander, multimedia and performing artist, trans woman, and all-around badass

The Long Term

We'll be looking at this in more detail in chapter 6, but, to put it briefly: we need better ways of navigating our long-term response to harassment and violence, especially at the community level.

We won't always know if the harm that people cause is accidental or intentional. Certainly we might choose to respond differently depending on which it is, but, either way, people who do bad things need not be exiled from our community in order to make things right. In this fucked-up world, the standard answer of what to do with such people is simple: punishment. But if our goal is a better, nonviolent society, don't we need better, nonviolent solutions? Obviously we cannot just banish our toughest cases or the worst among us, because we know they can move to another town where they will only continue their behavior. At the same time, the gargantuan prison-industrial complex we have now is a barbaric institution created by a barbaric society.

We must provide offenders with consequences for violent behavior *and* we must allow them the opportunity to learn how to do better. In terms of sexual harassment and assault, it is on us—the friends of the abuser, the friends of the victim, the community members—to do the difficult work necessary to make the community safer for all. We must help this person by holding them accountable until they can hold themselves accountable. While it is always best to follow the victim's lead, the community also has a right to ask this person to change their behavior in order to be given a second chance.

This book is addressed to spaces, and spaces occupy an important position in our communities. They are often the places where community happens. Or perhaps they occupy a middle ground where people gather in the process of building their wider community. As such, our spaces, our venues, and our community centers can play a crucial role in helping us find new ways to deal with unacceptable behaviors. Ultimately, it is our communities that have to decide. Until a harasser faces the consequences of their actions—whether that be therapy, community service, mediation, or an accountability process—there will be no change.

Callouts and What Comes Next

We are getting pretty good at the callout, especially online, where it's as easy as pressing a button. For those of you who don't know, the *callout* (sometimes generalized as *callout culture*) is a means by which harassers and abusers of all sorts have been publicly identified, denounced, and often shamed. It is, in certain ways, the engine behind the recent #MeToo movement and, as such, can be a useful tool for toppling serial creeps, even those with a lot of power. But it's only one tool in what should be a full toolbox.

The internet is great. While it's becoming more and more monetized with ads, bandwidth throttling, and other nasty business practices, it provides a somewhat open platform for people to make their voices heard. This is a good thing. On the flipside, it also divides us. We spend less time with people in person, especially people who think differently than us or have different beliefs. We can avoid such people online by creating a bubble of like-minded friends for ourselves, and the more of our social lives we spend online, the less we have to face anyone in the flesh. For progress to happen, though, we have to be ready to talk to people in person and challenge bullshit when we hear it. A 2016 study confirmed that speaking to people in person (in this case, as part of a door-to-door canvassing campaign) can actually have lasting effects on how someone thinks about an issue. Doubly exciting is that the study was done by following canvassers working in favor of transgender rights. Just a ten-minute conversation was able to "markedly reduce prejudice."[9] So, yeah, change is possible, and it starts with changing minds. Social media callouts might sometimes achieve that, but in-person communication has a better, and proven, track record. We don't have to use the same abusive tactics used by the creeps who abused us. We can be better than that.

The callout certainly serves a purpose in communities that don't want cops or the legal system involved. It can quickly and effectively make an abuser curtail their behavior, at least temporarily, but it is also an incomplete action. It stops short at public shaming, providing no resources for rehabilitation or healing. Lately though, a lot of people have begun wondering what do we do *after* the callout. This is a crucial question.

I believe those closest to people causing harm need to hold their friends or loved ones accountable until they can do so themselves. Confront them, talk to them, ask if they understand what they've done and how it affected people. Have they made that apology yet? Do they have a plan for making amends? Do they know what the victim wants for recompense? Do they need a liaison to communicate with the victim and ask? Have they contacted their local sliding-scale counseling center or joined a support group? Have they kept their word? These are all things *you* can ask or encourage to not

---

9   David Brockman and Joshua Kalla, "Durably Reducing Transphobia: A field Experiment on Door-to-Door Canvassing," *Science* 352, no. 6282 (April 8, 2016): 220.

only help your friend seek help but also to help their victims get justice, as well as help prevent potential future victims.

In a piece for the *Washington Post*, Rabbi Danya Ruttenberg addresses the #MeToo phenomenon of half-assed apologies from powerful men who seem to care more about hanging on to their power than what they did to abuse it.[10] The mainstream public is wondering exactly what should be done after someone says they are sorry. Is he truly sorry? Should we forgive him? Who is "we"? How long should he suffer? When can he be on TV again? Who decides any of this? It can be very confusing. But I found Ruttenberg's outline of what atonement really looks like helpful. "The Jewish tradition teaches that repentance is really hard work," she says, "in contrast to the glib and easy way these accused perpetrators are seeking cheap forgiveness from popular culture." She continues,

> America is often perilously quick to welcome comebacks, in part because we don't really know what it means to atone.... According to Jewish law, though, the most critical factor is repentance, *tshuvah*—the work that a person who has done harm must undertake. There are specific steps: The bad actor must own the harm perpetrated, ideally publicly. Then they must do the hard internal work to become the kind of person who does not harm in this

---

10 Danya Ruttenberg, "Famous Abusers Seek Easy Forgiveness. Rosh Hashanah Teaches Us Repentance Is Hard," *Washington Post*, September 6, 2018.

way—which is a massive undertaking, demanding tremendous introspection and confrontation of unpleasant aspects of the self. Then they must make restitution for harm done, in whatever way that might be possible. Then—and only then—they must apologize sincerely to the victim. Lastly, the next time they are confronted with the opportunity to commit a similar misdeed, they must make a different, better choice.[11]

Ruttenberg gives the example of a rabbi who, in atonement for his complicity in enabling a high school principal's sexually abusive acts, "has dedicated much of his life and work to advocating for victims of sexual assault."[12] Let's sit with that for a minute. Are you, as a club or gallery owner, as the collective that runs a social center where abuse or violence has happened, capable of such repentance or the sense of responsibility to others it implies? What are you capable of? What is your responsibility? No need to answer right away. Like I said, just sit with it.

Once the bad actor has done the serious work of becoming a better person, a community should let them back in, slowly of course, but still giving them a chance to continue doing right. It's okay to have some trepidation. Keep an eye on them, but do not be hostile. Not if they are trying to do the work. This is where the person who has harmed needs their friends and family the most.

11 Ibid.
12 Ibid.

None of this is easy. Not for the abuser and not for the abused and her community. As we'll see in chapter 6, simple eye-for-an-eye punishment is only one way of defining "justice." In the aftermath of trauma, that path might feel easier for victims and those around them. It gets the abuser out of sight and, theoretically at least, out of mind. But, if Rabbi Ruttenberg is correct, it might not be the best path to healing wounds, minds, or communities.

PART II

YOURSELF

What do all the spaces you inhabit have in common? You. Whatever space you're in, whatever role you play, you bring yourself into it. All your experiences, baggage, habits—good and bad. This half of the book is all about you: how to avoid harassing others and how to respond when others harass you. There are real-world examples of people just like you doing their best to create safer spaces.

four

HOW TO FLIRT WITHOUT BEING A CREEP

In 2017, my band, War On Women, went on the road with Vans Warped Tour. In addition to performing on stage, I taught a workshop called "Creating Safer Spaces." It was part of a series of workshops organized by The Education Institute (TEI), where artists and bands could connect with their fans on things that mattered to them in some way. Our new friend Lisa, for example, led a live photography workshop (and, right after, she'd sometimes lead an entire class directly in front of our stage to start taking photos of us—quite a sight!). There were lots of drumming or songwriting clinics, music-business-related roundtables, and sometimes purely fun stuff. I re-member the band CKY had a wheel of fortune that changed every day, so you could spin the wheel and potentially get to chug a beer with the bass player, make their roadie go get you a beer, or—something else beer-related, I don't know. TEI offered our band the opportunity to lead a workshop and it just made sense for me to share what I know about safer spaces with audience members all over the country.

As I envisioned it, the workshop was based on the street harassment and bystander intervention education work I was doing back home in Baltimore. For that, as I've mentioned, I go into venues of all kinds to talk about victim-blaming, crisis response, and the effects of harassment. I advise managers and staff on what to do if someone says they were harassed in their space. In other words, all the stuff this book is based on.

The trainings back home were addressed to the venues themselves. However, things were a little different on this tour. Most of the people I spoke with over the course of that summer identified as audience members—they didn't necessarily work for a club or play in a band. So I needed to adapt my usual shtick. Catering to this new audience allowed me to skip some of the advice that assumes my audience members are in positions of authority within the spaces we're trying to make safer. This left room for the workshop attendees to steer the discussion, exposing me to more perspectives and raising a different set of questions. Turns out a lot of people wanted to know how to flirt in a way that doesn't come across as harassment.

I get it. You see a cutie at the club or bar or basement show and want to interact, but with all this #MeToo stuff going on, you don't want to be accused of harassment. Good for you! Before I give you my "Dos and Don'ts of Healthy Flirting," I want you to think about something: when women and trans-gender and nonbinary folks say they're tired of harassment and assault, they are often met with a sentiment that boils down to, "So, what, I can't talk to women anymore?" Now this is a prime example of how our modern ideas of romance and sex are implicitly based on nonconsensual interactions. If you think you can't talk to me because I don't want to be harassed, what does that say about how you were planning on talking to me?

So, first lesson: the question isn't "How can I avoid being accused of harassment?" but rather "How can I avoid harassing someone?"

In order to avoid making people you're attracted to uncomfortable, you must work on recognizing the differences between flirting and harassment. You have to avoid victimizing behavior: just because someone looks good *to* you, it doesn't mean they're looking good *for* you or that they're asking for anything, including your attention. You also have to be ready and willing to call out your friends when you see them veering into harassment territory. No, this doesn't mean you can never talk to a woman again—it means you understand that she might live in a more threatening and violent world than you do. Sure, you might be a truly nice guy, but she doesn't know that. The best way to actually be a nice guy is not to tell her over and over; it's to show her. And, yeah, sometimes that means leaving her alone.

Maybe you've grown up with this idea that you have to win a woman by wearing her down until she gives in. This is pretty much the plot of most romantic comedies, certainly the ones I grew up watching in the eighties and nineties. Yes, every individual is different, but in general terms our culture teaches men to push, while women learn that their role is to push back. This is how very real social inequality and power differentials between genders translate into the "innocent" realm of romance and flirting. We've all internalized—and then reproduced—those social relations because, well, they're everywhere we look. But what if things looked different? What if we lived in a world where women's boundaries were respected? Where a polite "no" was heard and heeded? For one, you'd have more fun! I'd certainly be more open to chatting with a stranger at the bar if I knew I could say no at any time without negative repercussions.

Unfortunately, we don't live in that world—yet. Instead of being open to chatting with you and seeing where things go, I'm more likely to be wary and preoccupied, worrying about your ulterior motives, the possibility of a spiked drink, or planning my strategy for how to bow out of the conversation if things go south. I promise you: these are not sexy feelings!

When women and LGBTQIA folks are assaulted, followed, groped, or raped, they are often blamed for their own victimhood and questioned in a way that victims of other crimes are not. If your car is stolen, no one asks you how much you had to drink that night or what you were wearing. Men aren't even asked such questions if they were physically assaulted by someone. For marginalized folks, it becomes instinctual to do what we can to avoid these scary and potentially dangerous situations, because the support we need when things go wrong doesn't always exist. It's easier to protect ourselves by blowing you off, even if you're a perfectly nice guy. It's not about you. Truly nice guys get that.

That brings us to step one in respectful flirting: understand that if the person you're hitting on belongs to a group of people who are typically preyed upon by someone that looks like you, they may not want to risk opening a dialogue.

Once you've accepted that, really accepted it, read on for some pointers on interacting with strangers in public spaces. There's no point in reading them if you can't understand the basic premise that a woman can decide when the conversation is over. There's no convincing or "arguing your case." You don't have to win her over (which is the nice way of saying wear her down). Your desires end with you. The world and the people in it have no obligation to conform to them. Due to the messaging we've all received in our heterosexist patriarchal (I know, I know, but it's an accurate description) society, this is a fact many men and white people have a hard time understanding. But ignorance is not an acceptable excuse for hurting other people.

There's no such thing as a perfect game plan for this sort of thing. You can't learn a script for human interaction and have everyone follow it. What you can do is help build a world where women and members of LGBTQIA communities are not perpetually on guard, where we are free to have fun at a show without being harassed (accidentally or not). So…

First, just so we're on the same page about what flirting is: **There's no reason to tell a stranger what you think of their appearance**, especially if that is all you want to talk to them about. Trust me: they already know! The point of a compliment is to make the recipient feel good. Having strangers tell you (whether in flowery or vulgar terms) what they like about and what they want to do with your body does *not* feel good.

Unless you actually want their number, hope to date, or are raring to hook up, leave them alone. Remember, we're talking about flirting here. If you're *flirting* but not going to follow through, then you're leading them on at best, harassing them at worst. We live in a beauty-obsessed culture, but women especially are constantly judged by their "fuckability," always made to feel like a sexual object in public spaces (not a sexual subject, like men are). So they are not starved for strangers' attention or compliments! They're tired of being judged on their looks and worried about how far (i.e. physical) harassment will go. So they don't hear you say "You're really hot," they just hear "I'm a potential predator who wants to have sex with you." This might seem far-fetched, but by taking this example to the extreme, I hope to better demonstrate what it's like for people who aren't looking for attention. Admire them from afar (using the next rule) and just appreciate their existence.

Don't stare. I abide by a "two seconds or less" rule. If you want to stare, know that everyone else probably does too. This rule applies to anyone and everyone—people who are very tall, very short, very tattooed, or bear some other distinguishing feature are all tired of feeling like sideshows, even if some of these traits are chosen. If you accidentally catch their eye, a quick small smile and glance away is the least awkward move. Continuing to stare, or your eyes going wide with fear and turning your head so fast you get whiplash is, well, more awkward. If they meet that accidental glance with an "Eww, no" face, don't get mad. Just leave them alone and move on.

No racism, transphobia, Islamophobia, ableism, ageism, classism, fat-shaming, or homophobia allowed. Whatever obvious thing you were about to say about this person's appearance—they have heard it before, so even if they don't find it offensive, they will find it tired (as in, a turnoff). And trying to guess where someone "is really from" is racist. Got a fetish for whatever thing this person has going on? That's bedroom talk, not "I just met you" talk. Get to know *the person.* Then, if you ever make it that far, then you can share what you like about this *human being with their own thoughts and feelings.*

Read the situation. Are they with friends or deep in conversation? Are they zoned in on the show? Are they in the middle of ordering a drink? Respect context clues and don't interrupt their good time. If they're heading out, and you feel like you're losing your chance to meet the love of your life, you can say something quick and respectful. Calmly walk over to them, catch their eye (with a relaxed, gentle gaze) or give a light tap on the shoulder if necessary (is it necessary?), and say something like "Hey, sorry to bother you, I see you're on your way out with your friends. You just caught my eye back at the bar [at coat check, when you walked in]." As you say this, hand them a card or piece of paper with your name and number, and tell them "If you ever want to hang out, I'd be up for it; have a good night" and then walk away. If they were dying to talk to you too, then they'll stop you to chat more. If you piqued their interest, but they just don't have the time or energy to chat now, they'll contact you later. If they are not interested, they won't. You've told them how you feel in a respectful way and, now that your info is in their hands, the situation is out of yours. It's no longer about you.

Okay, they're free to talk, and you have more to say than "Hey baby, nice ass." **Don't talk about their body parts, what you want to do with them, or that one identifying characteristic that everyone probably talks to them about.** Talk about something they have control over. Like their shoes or hairstyle, maybe their jacket or what brought them to the show. Don't lie—I know you can come up with *something* to say. If this cutie has breasts, be wary of mentioning the band shirt they're wearing. Depending on the design, they might just think you're looking for an excuse to look at their chest. If you think you're being slick by taking quick-hit glances below the neck, trust me: we see it every time and you look like a doofus. Eyes up here, please.

Take the "no" with respect and grace. It's not always about you. They're just not interested, and there are about a million possible reasons why. A breezy "All good, I'll be at the table over there if you change your mind" shows confidence. Confidence is way sexier than desperation or anger.

Remember that there are many ways to say "no." Sometimes they're verbal ("No thanks," "I'm good," "Maybe next time," "Not tonight," etc.). Maybe it's a grimacing face, nervous laughter, or a shake of the head. Oh, is it frustrating that some women just won't say what they mean? Well, that's not nearly as frustrating as feeling unable to voice your discomfort for fear of your personal safety. If you encounter someone who's not comfortable saying a firm but polite no, it's probably because they don't know you or what you're capable of. Remember, we're living in a world where if I am attacked, I will be blamed in one way or another, so I've

How to Flirt Without Being a Creep

learned to protect myself by avoiding confrontation. If you take everything other than an enthusiastic "yes!" as a no, then you will never accidentally disrespect someone's boundaries.

Don't push someone to do something that they're not totally psyched about. Don't spike people's drinks. Don't get angry if someone says no. Don't follow people or stand too close to them or manufacture an excuse to touch them. Don't touch them unless explicitly and specifically invited to. Don't rape. If you don't think you can avoid any or all of these actions, then don't attend public gatherings without a buddy and promptly book a therapy session—this is something you need to work on. You cannot be a good partner (in or out of bed) to anyone if you have issues with boundaries, selfishness, narcissism, entitlement, anger, or if you believe that women owe you anything.

If any of these tips are new to you, please take time to analyze them from all angles and distances. Learn to recognize the difference between asking for someone's number and pressuring someone into giving you their number. Discuss these ideas with friends before they harass a stranger (accidentally or not) and definitely after.

Another point I'd like to make, one that I feel gets lost in these "But how do I even date now?" conversations, is the idea that you should focus on making yourself someone worth dating. Reading this book is a great start: you've got something to talk about at parties, skills to share with groups, and you've hopefully learned at least a couple new things about being a good ally to people who experience harassment. That's rad! You should also consider counseling or self-help books, practicing good communication skills with friends and coworkers, and joining a knitting circle/book club/DIY collective/some other cool local hobby group. Become the best person you can while waiting for your person to show up.

I've gone with the percentages here and have mostly assumed that person trying to find the line between flirting and harassment is male. Importantly, though, these tips are not just for men, and the person being flirted with doesn't have to be a woman. While statistics show that men are most often the perpetrators of gender-based violence and harassment, absolutely everyone deserves respect in public spaces—even if they are fucking hot. If you can be someone who others trust to respect boundaries, even at inconvenient times, people will feel a lot safer letting loose around you. You can feel good knowing that it's because they genuinely want to.[1]

---

1 This chapter is an expanded version of an essay that appeared on the *Revolver* magazine website on April 24, 2018.

five

WHAT TO DO IF YOU'RE BEING HARASSED

HARASSMENT CAN MAKE you feel scared, frustrated, angry, embarrassed, isolated, or all of the above. It can also make you feel very much alone. The truth is, though, however much it might feel otherwise at the time, you are *not* alone. In 2014, Stop Street Harassment commissioned a 2,000-person nationally representative survey in the United States.[1] The survey found that 65 percent of all women had experienced street harassment. Among all women, 23 percent had been sexually touched, 20 percent had been followed, and 9 percent had been forced to do something sexual.

---

1   Holly Kearl, *Unsafe and Harassed in Public Spaces: A National Street Harassment Report* (Reston, VA: Stop Street Harassment, 2014).

Anecdotally, most people would say those numbers are low—and we do know that most incidents of sexual assault go unreported, so we can reasonably expect that reticence carries over into surveys. In addition, while the statistics on other forms of harassment and identity-based violence are often lacking, it's a safe bet that comparable figures hold true for racial, transphobic, homophobic, classist, Islamophobic, and ability-based harassment. We do know, for instance, that 47 percent of transgender people are sexually assaulted at some point in their lifetime.[2] And 61 percent of Muslim Americans say they have experienced discrimination based on their religion in the past year.[3] We also know that levels of harassment and assault across the board are consistently higher for people of color and that the forms specifically designated as *hate crimes* have been on the rise.

So you are not alone in your experience of harassment, and you are probably not alone in the confusion and self-doubt you experience when trying to decide how to respond to it. Harassment is such a direct violation and diminishment of your very being that those of us who experience it often don't feel confident in the way we respond. We question ourselves in the moment and after the fact. But there's one important thing you should keep in mind: **there is no perfect response to harassment.** Each instance is unique enough that trying to respond in the exact "right way" each and every time will only add to your frustration. So let's

2   National Center for Transgender Equality, *Report of the US Transgender Survey, 2015* (Washington, DC: NCTE, 2015), 15.

3   Institute for Social Policy and Understanding, *American Muslim Poll 2018: Pride and Prejudice* (Washington, DC: ISPU, 2018), 15.

reduce the stress and talk about some immediate responses that might work for you.

In The Moment

First of all, ignoring it is a response, and it's a completely valid one. There's no reason to woulda/coulda/shoulda yourself after being harassed. You did not fail yourself, all womankind, or the queer community by walking away. Like anyone else, you deserve to go about your business as you please, and you do not owe anyone your time. So cut yourself some slack and reframe the act of ignoring someone as a power move.

Of course, sometimes ignoring it doesn't feel like the right thing to do, and you want to say something back. The problem is that the harassment itself can catch us off guard—no matter how many times it has happened in the past. That's why it's a good idea to plan a go-to response for such occasions. You don't have to use it, but it's nice to keep on hand. Simple statements like "Not interested" or "That's harassment" are good because they will work in a number of situations. They require almost no thought and, hey, why should you be wasting thought on someone who thinks harassment is okay?

Don't judge your reaction. We're trained from birth to be understanding and polite, especially to members of social groups with more social power, but it's important to realize that it's okay for you to make someone feel uncomfortable by telling them they are making you feel uncomfortable. You don't owe them your tolerance or sympathy. Stop prioritizing the feelings of someone using offensive language or gestures around you. They certainly weren't prioritizing your feelings when they said or did those things.

Stay calm. If we're on guard all of the time, it's easy for our brains to overload when a real instance of harassment occurs. "Is *this* the one that will turn violent?" Staying calm will not only help prevent the situation from escalating, it could also help you take a last minute emergency action if necessary. So take some deep breaths, take a moment to clear your head, and decide your next move. Your safety is paramount, so take care of yourself.

You decide when you are done, when the interaction is over. You don't owe strangers anything. Not your time, your attention, or your patience. It's not your job to cater to their expectations of what someone like you is supposed to do in this or any situation. If you have attempted to calmly let someone know how their comments make you feel, but they aren't letting up, it's fine to cut your losses and walk away. They may try to derail and redirect the conversation. They might become increasingly argumentative or even aggressive. Your physical safety and mental health are more precious than your harasser's feelings.

Relatedly, there's no need for you to argue or debate. If you feel like saying something then say your piece and move on. You are not likely to convince someone who's harassing you to see the error of their ways in that moment anyway. Most people with backward views are more likely to listen to and learn from someone who looks like them. They have already demonstrated a lack of respect for you—your opinions aren't any more likely to matter to them. And if they do take it to heart, it will likely be after your interaction is over, after some introspection. Focus on your own well-being and survival. Hopefully books like this and social movements like #MeToo will inspire more allies to make themselves known and take on these often frustrating conversations for you.

Assuming that women and people of color are responsible for educating their oppressors is just another layer of oppression.

Delegate. Remember the Five D's of Bystander Intervention in chapter 2? Well, this D works if you are a victim or a bystander. Ask the people around you to notice what is happening. Call it out specifically and directly: "This person has followed me for a block and is harassing me. They keep using homophobic slurs." Sometimes for a creep, knowing that others can see what they are doing is enough to get them off your back. But keep in mind: the people around you might want to help but not know how. So tell them. Again, be specific. Look someone in the eye and say "Can you record this lady yelling at me?" or "Can I stand next to you until that person leaves?" Even asking rhetorically "Can someone get this guy to leave me alone?" could inspire or encourage someone in hearing distance to come up with their own spontaneous intervention. If the person harassing you is with a friend or someone who is not participating in the harassment, delegate to them. You can say, "Hey, your friend is drunk and bothering me, can you walk them over there?" or "Get them out of my face before I tell security." Make it their problem. They are more likely to hold their friend accountable for any bad behavior if it affects them directly, so give them a job to do: move their friend away, get their keys, get them a ride home, or simply try to avoid making a scene.

It's the Behavior, Not the Person

Okay, here's where it gets a little complicated.

I've just told you that you don't owe your harasser much consideration or much of anything. But let's not confuse that with having a blank check to respond in ways that reproduce the same sorts of fucked-up biases and hierarchies that lead to other forms of harassment. We definitely *do* have a responsibility to avoid that.

Harassment is painful. It's frightening. There are many potential responses to feeling hurt or scared. Some people clam up. They refuse to think about it and may need a little extra help processing what happened to them, as well as help making sure they don't bottle up those feelings, letting them fester and perhaps cause more hurt in the long run. Others absorb the hateful messages, believing what society says about them being worthless or less-than. Working on a healthy self-image, building up your self-esteem, and setting good boundaries can help with these things, but there's no denying that the feelings involved can be ugly and that our responses might arise out of anger.

If your immediate instinct is to lash out, it's important that the coping skills you have developed do not involve the harassment or abuse of others. No matter what someone has said to you, it does not warrant using sexist, racist, homophobic, transphobic, ableist, Islamophobic, sizest, or classist language to insult or embarrass them. Their behavior toward you should be embarrassing enough: focus on that. To call someone out, to holla back at them, to name their behavior, to ask for help from bystanders—none of this should resemble harassment.

None of us lead "single-issue lives." As feminists of color have been pointing out for a long time, the laundry list of oppressions I often refer to in this book are *intersectional*, meaning they cross, combine, and compound one another, so that someone who is oppressed by one measure could be in a position of power by another.[4] That means you might have some power in a situation based on one identity while someone is trying to disempower you based on another. If you find yourself being more judgmental of your harassers when they don't look like you, or more forgiving when they do, it's important that you take a step back and analyze your responses. Are you letting the messaging of a white supremacist, patriarchal society influence how you perceive the actions of others?

Anyone can be a victim of harassment, just as anyone can be a harasser. But if you are reacting to the person harassing you more than to the harassment itself (if your knee-jerk reactions seem to be saying more about you than them), you might want to take the opportunity to unlearn your internal biases. Talk with a willing confidant, join an ally group, or read a few books that explain the struggles of other communities. Ultimately we're stronger when we're united, when our movements are as intersectional as our oppressions. Working to end one form of harassment can have a ripple effect as long as we don't let our unconscious biases undercut our positive efforts.

Victims and bystanders can have different roles when it comes to responding to harassment. Or at least bystanders often have the luxury of more distance. Victims are under no obligation to educate or be patient with someone causing them harm, while bystanders should feel that obligation. If you are a bystander and not directly affected, and you've

---

4   The concept of intersectionality came out of the work of the Combahee River Collective in the 1970s. For more on them, see Keeanga-Yamahtta Taylor, *How We Get Free: Black Feminism and the Combahee River Collective* (Chicago: Haymarket, 2017).

chosen to speak frankly with someone exhibiting problematic behavior, then talk about *the behavior and its effects*. Don't insinuate that they are a bad person at their core. One clear reason for this is that, when people feel unredeemable, they don't feel inspired to change! What's the point if they supposedly can't? So, instead of saying "You're a racist!" or even "Wow! That is *so* transphobic," you might try telling them that *what they said* was racist or letting them know that trans people generally find a particular word offensive, while offering them a better option.

Obviously, this only applies to times you consider it worth having a conversation—but I challenge you to reconsider what you find worth it. The key to effective communication is getting our point across, which means sometimes we alter our delivery depending on who we are talking to. This might be because we want to use words they will understand better, because we want to appeal to their better nature, or because we know we need to personalize an issue for them to care about it. You can even continue to think someone is a fucking racist while you work on getting them to be better at keeping it to themselves. This serves two purposes: it let's them know that not everyone who looks like them is okay with what they are doing or saying, and it can help prevent them from doing or saying those things around someone who would be directly offended, someone in the oppressed group that this person is prejudiced against. This might seem like a small victory, but we should take our victories where we can get them. Sure, there might be more glory in the big victories ("I just single-handedly shut down the Westboro Baptist Church thanks to my fact-based arguments, good looks, and charm!"), but that's not usually how change occurs. It happens incrementally on the individual level. Every time we get someone to take another step toward tolerance, they get that much closer to becoming a true ally. It's also good practice. Having these conversations when the (personal) stakes are low better prepares us for talking with our close friends and family.

Planning for Safety and Peace of Mind

Taking some control in a situation in which you feel helpless can help you process what you are going through faster and more fully. When you feel there is a pattern of anticipated or regular harassment, get out the pen and paper. Start making a list of all the things you can do, no matter how small, in the face of someone's shitty behavior. This is your safety plan.

It might, for instance, include all the logistics of avoiding the harassment in the first place. In real life, you could decide to change routes or the times you travel. Your virtual self might consider logging out of certain accounts for a some length of time, long enough for you to recover and reset. List the things you can get help with and the people you could ask to give it. Who can be your walking buddy? Who do you know in a position of authority who could make an announcement or otherwise use their platform? Who is good at organization and might help you avoid running into someone by (un)coordinating schedules?

Sometimes the help you need involves the upsetting task of documenting and processing instances of harassment. For online ugliness, you can get a friend to go through your messages for you and/or help you decide if you want to save, delete, or screen capture specific examples. You can also enlist the help of HeartMob, a Hollaback! project that offers private logs of online abuse, replies to the original harasser to call out the behavior, and/or gives support in the form of mobilizing other people online who can drown out any negative messages with positives ones.

When there are patterns of abuse or harassment, you don't have to decide right away how you want to handle it. Until you know if you just want it to stop or, for instance, will be taking it up with Human Resources, just start with documentation. A friend can also help by letting you email them all the details, including the date, time, and facts of situation, in order to establish a date stamp if you ever need proof or corroboration.

Another writing project would be to come up with what you see as the best possible outcome for your specific situation, no matter how outlandish it might be. Dig deep to figure out what it is you really want. Do you want to be removed from the situation? Do you want a public apology? For them to go to counseling? Or some other way to demonstrate they understand their behavior is wrong? Now figure out which elements on your wish list are achievable. Work toward what you can actually do, with or without the help of a friend. And when something positive does happen—even if it's just a coworker believing you when they are not in a position to help—celebrate that.

Sanity comes with action. Pen and paper help us organize our thoughts, but it's when we work to make ourselves and others safer that we start to feel relief and strength. I find that when I step up and intervene on other marginalized people's behalf, I feel empowered. It almost makes up for the many times I couldn't speak up for myself. So be an ally! It's good for your mental health and reminds you that you are not helpless.

More Creative Responses

Anyone who deals with harassment even semi-regularly has had plenty of experience gauging just how dangerous these situations can become. Being harassed is never your fault, and it's not on you to predict how aggressive or physical someone might be. There will be times when you know the best option is to get away as fast as possible. Trust your gut.

There will also be those times when you are not as worried about your physical safety and you're up for playing with this mouse like a cat. Those times may be few and far between, so feel free to have fun! You deserve a laugh. So when someone is acting a fool, act a fool right back. One cool thing about the anti-street-harassment community is how many badass, empowering, and just plain funny responses people have come up with to deal with harassment. A Google search is sure to provide more inspiration, but here are a few to get you started:

- Pick your nose at them.
- Announce that you just farted.
- When they ask to marry you, say "Yes, finally! I have a few kids I need help caring for. Hope you have a good job."
- Bellow "Whoooooooooo caaaaaaaaaaaares?!" like a giant foghorn.
- Repeat everything they say like a five-year-old.

- Dance like a chicken (à la the TV show *Arrested Development*).
- Sing your phone number to them (it just happens to be the same as the song "867-5309").
- If they tell you to smile, say "My dad just died."
- If they say "Lemme talk to you for a minute," start the countdown "60, 59, 58, 57, 56...",
- If they tell you you're "an ugly dyke," let them know you get more chicks than them.
- If they make fun of your hijab, say "Oh this? It's just hiding the serpents—or do you want me to turn you to stone?"
- If someone asks to touch your hair, ask if you can punch their face.
- If you're with a friend, pretend you don't hear or understand what your harasser is saying and have your pal repeat every bullshit thing they say in a very loud voice. Use your best imitation of Lil Jon's "WHAAAT?"
- Pretend they are someone you know. You: "Hey, Darryl, it's been so long!" Him: "I'm not Darryl, girl, I'm James, and I think you're sexy as hell." You: "Darryl, it's so good to see you! How's little Darryl? You still work at the graveyard, Darryl? Hey, Darryl, you owe me $500, remember?"
- Stare back. Keep staring. Don't break eye contact and make them feel weirded out for weirding *you* out!
- Physically get in their way until they acknowledge you. Don't let them get where they are trying to go until they apologize (or whatever reasonable thing you're asking them to do).

Creativity-wise, there are also endless, somewhat more artistic things you can try:

- Chalk walk: Put your message on the actual street for everyone to see! Whether you want to overwhelm a space with a message you wish they agreed with ("No Harassment Here" or "Harassment-Free Zone") or you want to warn the neighborhood ("This place harasses women" or "Don't give your money to racists"), it's a way to reclaim a space that you once felt demeaned in.

- Make a sign: Got some design skills? Worried chalk will wash off? Make a sign and post it around the neighborhood or outside of a business that needs to know it's not okay to bully anyone in your community. It can be serious and simple like the messages above, or it can be funny and tongue-in-cheek.

- Hand out cards: Handing out a business card is an easy way to end an unpleasant encounter. Only after you've walked away will they read "What you just said is harassment. Please do not say this to anyone else ever again" or whatever you decide to print on it!

There are so many ways women/femmes and nonbinary folks are harassed in the streets. Below are a few examples and how I handle each.

1. "Hey, Beautiful/ [Sexy, or some other unsolicited compliment]." This may seem benign, but it is not. The fact that the "Hey" (a normal salutation) is followed by a comment on your appearance is not okay! It also can easily escalate because the person already feels entitled to comment on your physical appearance. The best way to handle this is to simply pretend they do not exist. The real dangerous people will respond to your silence with "Bitch" or "You are not so pretty anyway." This shows you that this was not just a friendly hello!

2. "Smile." This also seems friendly but, again, the person is telling me what to do with my face. Usually I just start barking or twitching. It's way more entertaining than smiling anyhow!

3. Aggressive sexual language that is not solicited. I try to make eye contact with other people on the street and also, if need be, say out loud: "I do not know him." Many people will not get involved if they think it is a domestic issue, but if they know you are being harassed they will step in. If there is no one on the street, I try to walk in the path of the light and pull out my phone and call someone so the harasser knows they will be held accountable for their behavior (i.e., there is a witness).

One time, when I was performing, I hopped into the audience, and a man grabbed my ass. I looked at him and loudly said, "Do not touch me without my permission." If I feel safe (I did because I was in a huge crowd), I call them out directly. They need to know that touching someone without their permission is never acceptable. And also: public shaming works. Most of the time these men *behave this way because they do not feel they will be held accountable for their behavior.*

—Shanthony Exum, aka Miss Eaves,
rapper extraordinaire

When You're Harassed in a Venue

In earlier chapters, I addressed venues directly, telling them how to respond when someone has been harassed in their space. I've also touched on what audiences and bystanders can do. What about when you are personally harassed in a venue? What can you do?

Asking that question isn't about giving the venue a pass, especially if their policies (or lack thereof) have contributed to the situation or even made it worse, but anyone can make a mistake. Even well-intentioned people who want to help might draw a blank when trying to imagine how. You can't control their response, but you can control your behavior. Here are a few tips that might help reporting harassment in a venue go a little more smoothly.

If a venue has signage suggesting they care about safer spaces, you should feel comfortable talking to anyone about what you just experienced. Unless their policy specifically states who to tell, it doesn't hurt to ask a staff person, "Who's the best person here tonight to talk to about some harassment I just experienced?" This allows them an out if they are too distracted or untrained to help you. You *want* them to have an out if they aren't able to deal effectively; this can lessen your overall trauma in the long run by reducing the chance of them making things worse.

Once you find a friendly ear, calmly tell them what happened, where, by whom, and what you need to feel safer in that moment. Maybe you just need to sit near security, maybe you need an escort to your car, maybe you need them to kick the harasser out, maybe you just want them to talk to the creep or keep an eye on them. Whatever it is, tell them. It might be tough to do this, to clearly express your needs to a stranger, but even people who want to do the right thing—including those who have gone through training and "done the right thing" before—are human, imperfect, and can misstep. As best you can, be clear about what you need. Don't take offense if they didn't offer it first. No one's a mind reader. In the moment, if you are too flustered to even know what you need, don't sweat it! Don't add self-criticism to your problems. Confusion is a natural response to harassment, and it's acceptable to say just that: "I'm overwhelmed right now, can I just stand here?" Take your time, let them bring you back to the present with grounding techniques if that's what you need, and give them a chance to make the situation right.

It's understandable that if you're harassed in a venue that does not claim to be a safer space or has no obvious signage to suggest they are, you might not trust them to help you. Frankly, that is why I co-created the Safer Spaces Program in Baltimore: we knew that people who live with the constant threat of violence are not always able or willing to speak up during an incident. But it's also important to understand that you're not obligated to! If you want to leave, that is perfectly reasonable. I suggest that after some time passes and you feel calm about the situation, reach out to the club—tell them what happened, and that you didn't know who you should tell, and see what their response is. Maybe they'll prove to you that they can't handle your truth, but maybe they'll surprise you. If they seem shocked at what occurred, apologetic, and encourage you to report next time, you can help them improve their response for the next person harassed by suggesting they put up obvious signage and post their policies publicly. You don't have to do the work for them, but any time we help an individual or group become more victim-centered in their responses, we help future victims. Remember, helping others is empowering. And sometimes easier than helping ourselves. It's a way to pay positivity forward, to build trust in the community. Trust is reciprocal, and keeping the communication open is the best way for people to actually hear suggestions on how they can improve without feeling defensive and shutting down.

If you've tried to communicate directly with the venue (tried to find the right person to talk to, clearly communicated what happened and what needs to happen in response), but they seem totally unapologetic or dismissive, then you hereby have my permission to go the public shaming route. Tag them or tweet at them, keep it factual, and either end it with a reasonable ask, or, if you're done and never want to go back and don't even care if they change their ways at this point, then leave it as a warning to others who might not want to spend their money there. A couple things to note: there is a difference between a venue that did not respond well to your complaint of harassment and a venue that encouraged or participated in your harassment. You can feel as angry as you want at either situation, but your public response might need to be tailored appropriately. Enlisting the help of all your followers and publicly calling for a ban of a venue before trying to talk directly with them? Let's save that for the venues with sexist or racist imagery all over their walls, stupid signage on the tip jars, staff that directly harassed you, and management that shrugs it all off—not the venue that usually tries their best but maybe didn't perfectly respond to you on a busy night. Not because you don't deserve to feel safe or get justice. You do. But getting people to change and improve begins by acknowledging that they are capable of just that. Just wanting to let the world know "this place sucks" changes nothing. I don't think you're that kind of person, though, if you've gotten this far into this book.

Responding to Harassment Online

"Don't feed the trolls" might be a good personal mantra for dealing with online harassment, but it's not necessarily great advice for everyone. Online harassment sits on the continuum of identity-based violence and its effects. According to the HeartMob website:

> Online harassment includes a wide range of targeted behaviors, including threats, repeated hateful or discriminatory messages, publishing personal information (doxxing), DDoS attacks, swatting, non-consensual sharing of intimate images ("revenge porn"), defamation, and even directly promoting harm. Online harassment can target—or come from—a group or individual. It often has the expressed purpose of forcing the target to abandon the internet or take down their content. While there is space for debate and discussion online (as well

as conflicting ideas!), what separates online harassment from healthy discourse is the focus
on harm: including publishing personal information, sending threats with the intention
to scare or harm, and even directly promoting
harm against a person or organization.[5]

In a world where staying offline is not really an option,
marginalized people are going to come across some online
hate no matter how curated their feeds are. The idea that you
can somehow avoid online harassment by staying off your
device is just as silly as the idea that you can simply avoid
street harassment by staying home. You have the right to live
your life, online and off. But just because you can expect harassment doesn't mean you have to accept it. And you're not
alone. HeartMob refers to a Pew Research Center survey that
found that 40 percent of people have been harassed online
and 66 percent had witnessed someone else being harassed
online.[6] Fifty-eight percent of these incidents happened on
a "social networking site or app."[7] As with all forms of harassment, we know that the online sort is widespread, but
that women, people of color, and LGBTQIA folks experience
more of it, especially when it comes to actual threats. But
whether you are a victim of online harassment or a bystander,
you have options.

---

5   "Social Media Safety Guides," HeartMob, https://iheartmob.org/
    resources/safety_guides.
6   Maeve Duggan, *Online Harassment 2017* (Pew Research Center,
    2017), 3.
7   Ibid., 81.

It's always a good idea to document *any* instance of abuse or harassment. You never know when you'll need it, so take screenshots of everything and put them away in a folder you don't have to look at all the time. This includes personal or public messages, as well as any time you have told someone about the harassment. Build that paper trail—in the virtual and the real world. If you ever decide that going to the cops is the right course of action for you, have a printed version of all your screen grabs in addition to a USB key or hard drive with all the information. Considering how slow the law is to catch up with technology, and the variations in laws by state, the more you can help your case, the better.

Proactive steps to online safety include enabling two-step verification, strengthening passwords, searching for yourself on "people finder" websites (and requesting they remove any sensitive information), and limiting what you share in the first place. When you're being harassed, online or off, it is not your fault, and you can respond however you like. You can just ignore it, you can engage the harasser(s) by standing your ground or explaining why what they are doing is hurtful, you can block them or report them to the site you're using, and you can expose them by reposting those screen grabs to put the lens back on their bad behavior where it belongs. Whatever you decide to do, it's your choice, and you can disengage whenever you want.

Bystanders to online harassment will usually have the most impact not with the original harasser but with other bystanders who might not perceive the person's abusive behavior for what it is. The more you can demonstrate for the crowd that a racist or transphobic comment is not cool, the better. You're not only letting others know that not everyone agrees with this jerk, you're also showing victims that they're not alone and that someone has their back. That's huge. So don't ignore it: state your case and try to persuade where you can. If they're just not giving you an inch, then you can expose them (by reposting their comments), report them, and then block them.

There's a lot of information out there about protecting yourself, so to better learn about all your options, read up on HeartMob and Crash Override. HeartMob is a platform that provides real-time support to individuals experiencing online harassment while empowering bystanders to act. It lets you report and document harassment across platforms and get the kind of help you want from the community, because victims can ask for exactly what they need, when they need it. The goal is to reduce trauma for people being harassed online by giving them what they feel will aid them the most in weathering the storm.[8] Crash Override, in their own words, "is a crisis helpline, advocacy group, and resource center for people who are experiencing online abuse. We are a network of experts and survivors who work directly with victims, tech companies, lawmakers, media, security experts, and law enforcement to educate and provide direct assistance working to eliminate the causes of online abuse."[9]

Self-Care

"Caring for myself is not self-indulgence, it is self-preservation, and that is an act of political warfare." This quote

---

8   Heart Mob, https://iheartmob.org.

9   Crash Override, http://www.crashoverridenetwork.com.

from Audre Lorde is well known for a reason: it resonates. Maybe you are stretched too thin taking caring for your kids, an elderly parent, or a sick loved one. Maybe you have too many jobs and not enough money, or your activism and local community work occupy all your free time. Or perhaps you have experienced abuse or violence and need to heal from that trauma. Whatever your situation, you are no good to anybody if you aren't healthy. So think of taking time for yourself. You're not quitting or abandoning your team but rather taking the bench for a little while, as long as you need. Rest up, let the other players get some field time, and come back ready to kick some ass yourself.

"Self-care" is one of those terms whose meaning has been watered down a lot in this internet age. While it's common these days to say that buying yourself that pumpkin spice latte is self-care, that's not the original intent of the phrase (and this is coming from a die-hard PSL fan, so you know I'm serious). Self-care is not an excuse to be a selfish jerk to other people. Sure, sometimes you might need to cancel plans to take care of yourself, but self-care does not mean you get to be flaky or late all the time. It's a mindful practice for health and well-being, not an excuse.

Sometimes a drink to take the edge off is a form of self-care (hello, 2016 election!), but sometimes it's recognizing and doing something about the fact that your drinking is interfering with your life and preventing you from being your best self. Sometimes self-care is cutting a toxic person out of your life, and sometimes it's learning how to deal with difficult people. Sometimes it's telling the people closest to you how they can help you through this rough time, but sometimes it's getting structured or professional help to ensure you

IDEAS FOR PRACTICING
SELF-CARE

PHYSICAL
go for a walk
dance
hike
swim
get a hug
play with a dog
clean and re-organize
your room
take a bath

EMOTIONAL
meditate
practice yoga
light a candle
talk with a friend
go on a date
journal
write down a list of things
you're grateful for

MENTAL
read a book
learn a new skill like
photography or drawing
do a DIY project
color
turn off your phone

From the blog of Dr. Harmeen Bhatia
http://drharmeenbhatiashomoeopathy.com/blog/
ideas-for-practicing-self-care/

don't burden those you love unnecessarily or more often than they can handle. Self-care is not a product you can buy on the capitalist market; it's not a neurotic self-improvement project. It is about taking a break from what breaks you, nourishing your mind and body, unplugging and recharging, and preparing yourself to reenter the world.

Get out that pen and paper again. What are your favorite self-care practices? Write them down here for easy reference the next time you need them:

six

THIS IS WHAT
JUSTICE LOOKS LIKE

Real-World Examples

ANOTHER WAY OF looking at safety—from harassment or other forms of harm that humans cause—is through the lens of justice. In fact, some notion of implicit or explicit justice runs through most of what we've talked about so far. Justice can be about what happens after harm has occurred: the reaction, the redress, the repair. It can also be about building strong, just communities in which harm is less likely. The best solutions to harassment and violence are ones that keep both in mind. This chapter will try to trace a path through various options, explaining a few different models of justice and conflict resolution—enough so you can hopefully decide what might work best in certain situations, allowing you to dive deeper into those methods when you need them. I will also share some real-world examples from people invested in safer spaces.

After the Harm: Violence and Nonviolence

Mainstream society is just starting to ask the right questions regarding what happens after harm has been caused. We worked so long to get the general public to accept the seriousness and pervasiveness of identity-based violence, but, as soon as our society started to get it, we got defensive. Instead of sitting with the pain and in the discomfort of our role in upholding a culture that silences victims and lets people who harm walk free, instead of looking to those with experience and wisdom to ask what we could do to help, we've done no soul searching. We impatiently want to skip several steps, hoping to jump to the end of a redemption-story arc, where victims would forgive and forget so quickly that no one would need to bother doing the actual work of redemption in the first place.

We demand that victims and their advocates tell us what to do. Or we jump to the other extreme, throwing up our hands at the seeming impossibility of undoing so much injustice, asking "Are we just supposed to put every white man in jail now?" While the answers aren't going to come easily, giving up isn't an option, at least not for those of us on the receiving end of oppression. There is no single response to violence in our communities. Each instance is unique and nuanced, so our approaches should be too. Victims or their loved ones might call for vengeance. Disbelievers might call for evidence, police reports, and criminal cases. People not directly affected and who don't understand the gravity of the situation might think we can all just sit down and talk out our differences.

Luckily, the crucial work of creating methods that encourage actual resolutions (that do not involve the racist justice system) is already underway. Like most so-called radical ideas about what marginalized people need to end the violence against them, much of the research and implementation of these tactics has already been done and proven. We just need to listen and follow suit. And make sure that others listen.

Strangely, the biggest hurdle for most people is the very basic idea that no one is disposable—even people who have caused harm. It's strange, in part, because many of the people who can't get their heads around it are the same people who, in theory, believe that prisons should be about rehabilitation and healing and that there are serious problems with our criminal "justice" system. Maybe this isn't so surprising though: it's easier to feel compassion for abstractions than it is for someone who has just hurt us or someone we love.

A lot of the harm we're talking about in this book has been inflicted by individuals who would be called "good people" by their friends and family, people who have "always been nice to me" or who volunteer on the weekends and call their mom every Sunday. They are complicated human beings, capable of doing good and bad things, just like the rest of us. They are us. Because our society has for so long treated victims with disdain, it makes sense that women's rights activists have been figuratively shouting "Believe victims!" from the rooftops. However, it is possible to support and believe victims while also allowing an accused person the space to take responsibility for their actions, unlearn their abusive tendencies, and potentially go on to become an ally in the fight for a less violent world.

Jumping immediately to the retribution option is not always the best idea. A common mistake made by people who weren't directly affected by the problematic or abusive behavior in question is to circumvent the victim and come up with their own definition of justice. This can be unhelpful for a host of reasons, but to me the most damaging is the fact that it diminishes a survivor's autonomy. To publicly talk shit about the accused, for example, can very easily make the situation worse for the victim(s). It could effectively out them, putting their trauma up for public consumption and scrutiny. They might not be ready to process what they're going through, let alone with an audience. And if they are working with close allies to get a plan together to address what has happened to them, you might tip their hand or cause them undue stress during the process. Using the Ring Theory discussed in chapter 3, it's better to back off and ask the person one ring in from you how you can best be of help during this time.

Another reason to take a victim's wishes into account when it comes to deciding what justice looks like is that violence begets violence. It's almost a stereotype that any cisgender men who are friends/partners/family members of a sexual assault victim will be inclined to default to violence as a solution. Obviously, jumping someone or punching them out will contribute to the violence of the situation, but even the threat of that violence could ricochet back to the victim. It's likely that if the accused feels threatened or is actually harmed, they will blame the victim and could take revenge on them. The entire point of the tactics laid out in this book is to help create a less violent world. We can't do that if we solve our problems with violence, even when they are violent problems.

Bottom line: do not assume to know what is best for the victim of hate- or identity-based violence. Not only are they the ones who know best for them, but retaining some control after something harmful has been done to them is an important part of the healing process.

As mentioned in chapter 2, victims often experience secondary traumatization. Let's help them avoid that by allowing them to deal with one trauma at a time. Your role is to support a victim through a tough time, not decide guilt or innocence—or punishment. Help them reclaim some of the power that was just stolen from them by letting them take the lead on what to do next. What you can help with is giving them some realistic choices and letting them decide.

A commonly overlooked choice can be some version of transformative justice.

We're trained to think that the justice system is always fair and always gets it right, but that is far from true. Study after study shows that the crimes of rape and sexual assault have some of the lowest conviction rates, that people with black and brown skin, but especially Black men, are convicted of nearly all crimes at a higher rate than white men, and the news keeps showing us stories of women being assaulted while in police custody and undocumented women being assaulted in ICE detention centers. Simply the idea that there is such a thing as for-profit private prisons should be a red flag to us that the justice system isn't interested in a less violent society at all. But a less violent society is possible. It is not unrealistic or an unattainable utopia. It takes work, but it's worth it if it means keeping families together, normalizing tolerance, consent, and kindness, and preventing further harm. In fact, there are many groups and communities working out experiments, pushing forward, and building the framework for what this alternative form of justice could look like.

A Community-Led Confrontation

Maybe the best way to think through some of this stuff is to dive right into one of my own attempts. This all happened before I'd done much research into alternative forms of justice, so it's a good example to learn from. I think we did a good job, even without the theory to back it up.

A few years ago, a string of spiked drinks around Baltimore put everyone in my scene on edge. They were hitting all our favorite places—the bars and clubs we felt comfortable in— and my bartender friends were understandably stressed but doing their best to stay hyper-vigilant. One night Daphne, a bartender at Bar X, complained of getting drunk really fast from one drink and told her coworkers she suspected Jake.[1] Jake was a regular, and he'd been observed by staff touching women's drinks, knocking into women, tipping drinks to encourage women to drink faster, inappropriately touching women (being a little too friendly with strangers), leering, and generally being a creep.

Even though no one could say for sure that he had drugged Daphne's drink, he was there that night and in the context of this dangerous summer, his actions were suspect. When you

---

1 The names in this story have been changed for privacy and safety.

added them up, all his little behaviors seemed intentionally harmful, even if, on their own and witnessed by different people at different times, the case to ban him wasn't strong. He hadn't been caught doing anything illegal, and management was reluctant to kick him out permanently without a trusted eyewitness account of an illegal activity.

Fed up and wanting the behavior to stop, a group of women and nonbinary folks decided to take matters into their own hands. That's where I come in. They asked me to join them to meet up in person and discuss the specifics of Jake's behavior and talk about options. After meeting with this small group, I wrote up a plan based on their knowledge of events and their actionable goals. They wanted to confront Jake.

The goal of the confrontation was to inform him about how others viewed his behavior, to have him hear how others were affected by it, and to encourage him to change. We also wanted to let him know that as long as he was able to change his ways, he would be allowed to continue his social interactions at Bar X. This group was confident someone else in the scene would use violence against this man if he kept engaging in harmful behavior at public bars. This was their effort to reform him. They agreed that they'd rather he stay local and change his ways, than move away in order to avoid threats to his physical safety, only to engage in the same harmful behavior against others in another town.

Looking back, I know to call this a community-led confrontation. How a victim (or a victim's advocate) might confront someone who has harmed would be a different process with different goals. In our case, everyone involved in the process was either a suspected target, a potential future target, or a concerned community member with a stake in how it played out, due to their relationship with the bar and their responsibility toward its patrons.

Our first step was to inform the bar's management of our plan and ensure that all staff knew to hold off on getting involved because there was a group of women and nonbinary people handling the situation. We wanted to be sure we had full autonomy and respect while pursuing a nonviolent confrontation.

Next, we prepared a written response in case the confrontation went poorly, so everyone concerned could react in real time as a united front. If things went south, we would be able to send a quick message to Bar X's management and staff telling them to ban Jake from the bar before he had a chance to show up there. The third step was, through our safety networks, to inform bar staff around the city of Jake's activities and the general outline of our plan. We thought this could lead to more witnesses coming forward. We reasoned that, even if Jake had never drugged anyone, his general creepy behavior had made women feel uncomfortable and it deserved to be kept track of.

I helped turn everyone's ideas and desires into an actionable plan, and our friend Lauren was elected to do most of the talking in the confrontation itself. I would be there as a (mostly) silent support person. Lauren's calm demeanor, lack of previous one-on-one interactions with Jake, and relationship to the bar as well as knowledge of de-escalation techniques, made Lauren the perfect choice for this role.

We messaged Jake online to say that we represented a small group of people that had a community concern that affected him. We kept it vague and simple, assuring him we just wanted to talk but that we felt it was important he hear from us. Luckily for us, he agreed to meet. Lauren and I met up early to go over our notes together, ensuring we were on the same page about content and tone. Talking through what we wanted to say really helped keep our points factual, direct, and succinct.

We had encouraged Jake to bring his own *support person* to the meeting, which we held in a public coffee shop. We started by making it clear that we didn't actually know if he'd spiked anyone's drinks, but his other behaviors were making people suspicious. We told him what those behaviors were; he was invasive of people's space—specifically women's space— sometimes being too touchy or handsy with them; he'd been seen touching other people's drinks, which, even if it was accidental, didn't come across well; on multiple occasions, people seemed suspiciously intoxicated after interacting with him; he misinterpreted women's politeness for consent or interest; in general he was making people feel uncomfortable.

We knew just saying what he was doing wrong was not enough, that we needed to provide alternative behaviors for him to demonstrate. So we told him what we wanted him to do instead: be aware of how your actions affect others around you; stop staring at people; stop touching people's drinks; stop touching people without asking (because women are raised to be polite even when they are uncomfortable, you must obtain explicit and enthusiastic consent before touching, grabbing, or kissing anyone); stop asking us to marry you; consider therapy; read a book about boundaries and consent. We had a card up our sleeve to play if he was overly defensive or dismissive or aggressive: if he did not stop these behaviors, he not only wouldn't be allowed into several different establishments around the city, but we also could not guarantee his safety.

While he denied ever engaging in any of the behaviors we had listed, or at least claimed to be unaware of them, he did listen and take in what we said. It is common for someone who has been called out for harmful behavior to deny the allegations or play dumb, so we expected that. But we also knew he would know the community was watching him, and that we wouldn't put up with that behavior from him anymore. We kept it calm, and we let him save face. Our goal was not to be right or put on a dramatic show for the table next to us. The goal was only to have him change his behavior to keep our community safe. I don't think Jake ever became a feminist ally marching on the front lines, but he did stop bothering women at Bar X. When he would see Lauren out in public for a while, he seemed a little uncomfortable, perhaps embarrassed, which is a natural response that shows promise. No one on our side was working to actively shame him after the confrontation, and he's been free to participate socially ever since. We've not had any reason to confront him again.

Restorative and Transformative Justice

Our homemade approach worked and, however small a difference we made, it still had an impact. How many women's nights out have been made better by getting that one guy to check his behavior? When I look back at it now, on the other side of my research into harassment and sexual assault, I can see that our approach had a number of elements used by community accountability models of justice. It relied on the basic principles of transformative justice, even if that's not what we called it.

The two main models of alternative justice practiced today are known as *restorative* and *transformative* justice. The terms are often used interchangeably because there is a lot of overlap between them, but for our purposes transformative justice takes the basics of restorative justice a little further.[2] Both see crime as more than a single act that breaks a law. It is also something that harms both individuals and communities, and *justice* is the attempt to somehow repair that harm. Restorative justice can take place within or outside the existing criminal justice system, but prison is not its goal. It involves some form of mediation between the victim and the abuser aimed at negotiating a solution that both parties agree to. The goal is to somehow repair the harm done by getting the abuser to understand what they did, take responsibility for it, provide some form of restitution, and not do it again. It seeks to *restore* a previous equilibrium. Transformative justice, as I use the term, does much of the same but also understands that the former equilibrium may not have been particularly just to begin with and therefore seeks to *transform* both the individuals and the social context in which the harm became possible.

State-run models of justice are inherently punitive. When someone is found guilty, they "pay their debt to society" and

---

2 For a good overview of the various ways people understand the differences and similarities between restorative and transformative justice, see M. Kay Harris, "Transformative Justice: The Transformation of Restorative Justice," in Dennis Sullivan and Larry Tifft, eds., *Handbook of Restorative Justice: A Global Perspective* (London: Routledge, 2006).

we consider the matter resolved. This process effectively leaves out the victim's wishes, the potential growth or rehabilitation of the person who caused harm (essentially reducing people to one or few of their actions), and it ignores the circumstances that lead to the harm in the first place—which in all likelihood are still there after "justice" has been carried out. It also assumes that whoever decides the final verdict of guilt or innocence is always right. In a criminal justice system focused so intently on winning, the definition of harm remains dangerously narrow, an either/or scenario in which broader social and community needs disappear.

So much of the harm caused in everyday life is relatively minor and persistent. How can we realistically deal with everyday harm, the kind not addressed or even taken seriously by a punitive justice system? We didn't want Jake to go to jail for leering. But if his behavior wasn't put in check, if he didn't show remorse for crossing other people's boundaries, then research shows he could easily commit more severe transgressions, resulting in much more serious harm to others or others seeking vigilante justice against him.[3]

When left unchecked, harmful behavior can get worse. Locking someone away doesn't get to the root of the problem.

---

3   "Men who rape tend to start young, in high school or the first couple of years of college, likely crossing a line with someone they know, the research suggests.... Some of these men commit one or two sexual assaults and then stop. Others—no one can yet say what portion—maintain this behavior or even pick up the pace." Heather Murphy, "What Experts Know about Men Who Rape," *New York Times*, October 30, 2017, https://www.nytimes.com/2017/10/30/health/men-rape-sexual-assault.html.

Punishment is a short-term, superficial solution to bad behavior. In that sense, transformative justice is proactive, as it can prevent future victims. It actually addresses harm that is often overlooked by state-run punitive systems; it is responsive. When a resolution is agreed upon that does not include jail time, the root cause of the problem is still being addressed even without the usual, recognizable punishment of incarceration.

Does it really make sense to avoid society's maladies by locking up and forgetting the people that remind you of them? Sure, the alternatives are harder to do. They require looking at someone holistically, knowing that they weren't born bad, and understanding that they may have been victimized in various ways too. For the perpetrator, it takes work to get people in the same room, allow them both to tell their side, and work with everyone to reach a resolution that feels like justice to the people involved. It's work to take a hard look at yourself, seek treatment or help for your issues, and replace bad habits with good ones. It is also difficult work for the victim to forgive the person who harmed them, or at least not want to lock them away forever and accept that they can become a better person.

So let's consider how some groups have approached these difficult questions.

Community Conferencing

There is an organization in my hometown called Restorative Response Baltimore. Its members practice a type of *community conferencing* that is a good example of a basic form of restorative justice. They offer their service to schools, workplaces, and communities as a "process that includes everyone involved in and affected by an incident, crime, or conflict, and their respective support networks."[4] Meetings are led by an "all-partial" facilitator, and the meetings they lead provide "participants the opportunity to discuss 1) what occurred, 2) how they were affected by it, and 3) ways to repair any harm and move forward so that it does not happen again."[5] The idea is that the effects of harm are felt by the entire community and that the community itself should help come up with a way to move forward.

The ultimate goal is for people to resolve conflicts on their own, with the assistance of trained mediators who help to provide the structure in which dialogue happens and to facilitate healthy communication.

Clearly, the traditional setup of, say, a room full of neighbors discussing what happened and how it affected them does not work well when it comes to sexual assault. The violation and harm involved is a little different than a mere squabble about graffiti or even burglary. There is no scenario where *forcing* a victim to sit down with her attacker in front of a crowd and talk it out is going to work. Still, the abuser's necessary work of atoning for gross sexual misconduct should be done whether or not the victim wants to be involved in that process. What that absolutely requires, victim involvement or not, is for the accused to take responsibility for what they've

---

4   Restorative Response Baltimore, "Addressing Conflict through Community Conferencing," Restorative Response Baltimore, https://www.restorativeresponse.org/conferencing.

5   Restorative Response Baltimore, "Restorative Practices," Restorative Response Baltimore, https://www.restorativeresponse.org/restorative-practices/.

done. This is often done without cops or a goal to litigate—by design! The point is not to put people in jail but to heal the community by changing bad behavior and building trust. So owning up to actions, while your lawyer might advise against it, is the only way to get through a process like this.

Let's look at a few approaches to *transformative* justice that specifically address sexual violence. While reading, think of a specific conflict known to you, whether you're directly involved or not. How might these different methods serve your situation? What would be most appropriate? Would any get you to a resolution that works for everyone?

INCITE!

INCITE! is a group held in very high regard in conversations about transformative justice. Their work of reliably documenting alternative justice methods over the last couple decades is often referenced and, rightfully, considered an important pillar of the movement. Led by and focused on women of color to address sexual violence, INCITE! has a deep understanding of why the state and its police force do not always have a victim's best interests in mind and why it's worth repairing communities from within.

To say that INCITE!'s analysis starts from a holistic, macro understanding of violence is something of an understatement. They see harassment and assault of women and LGBTQIA people not only as a form of violence but also as part of an overall project of gender oppression.[6] They are

---

6   INCITE! Women of Color Against Violence, "Community Accountability within People of Color Progressive Movements: Selections from the 2004 Report," in Ching-In Chen, Jai Dulani, Leah

unambiguous about the cultural practices that keep that oppression in place and shield abusers from being held accountable. This clear-eyed view of the ugly structural forces we face is in part what leads them to suggest transformative justice as a solution: the rules of the game itself have to be changed if violence is to be stopped. Otherwise, we're just continually treating symptoms without addressing causes.

INCITE! believes that collectively we have more options (and more power) than we do individually. That community-level perspective does not prevent them from knowing that a survivor's safety is paramount in any accountability process. In a 2004 report, they address survivors directly. The list of their advice for survivors is worth sharing in full:

1. It is not your fault. The abuse is the responsibility of the perpetrator and/or the organization allowing the abuse to occur.

2. Think about what you want for safety and healing. Safety and an opportunity to heal from oppression and abuse are your right. Think about what you need from your friends, family, coworkers, comrades, your organization, and the movement for safety and healing. Do you want additional support? Should your organization be providing leave time? Support for counseling? A space for you to be heard?

3. Think about the role of the organization in addressing accountability and reparations. Accountability

Lakshmi Piepzna-Samarasinha, eds., *The Revolution Starts at Home: Confronting Intimate Violence within Activist Communities* (Oakland: AK Press, 2016), 281.

for oppression/abuse is different for different people, for different situations. Do you want a statement of accountability and apology? Do you want it made public? Do you want it written? Do you want a supportive space for your abuser to hear and understand what you have experienced? Do you want a public statement from your organization?

4. Think about how you want to be involved in the process of accountability. Do you want to be involved in every step? Do you want to be involved in specific aspects of the process? Do you want to stay out of the process but be informed at certain times, regarding certain decisions?

5. Think about how you want to communicate with the perpetrator. Do you want to face the perpetrator in person? Alone? With other support? If you face the perpetrator in person, do you want that person to remain silent? Do you want to give them an opportunity to respond? In person? In writing? Will you accept communication only if it is in the form of apology and accountability?[7]

They provide similar advice for the survivor's supporters, as well as for abusers and their supporters. The advice for the latter two, however, revolves around accepting responsibility and making amends, not making excuses, preparing their defense, or expecting anything from the survivor. And, importantly, they also (in a separate document) address the responsibilities a community has in preventing the conditions under

7   Ibid., 288.

which inequality and abuse thrive. They define "community" broadly as "a group of friends, a family, a house of worship, a workplace, an apartment complex, a neighborhood, and so on," and they recommend that each proactively:

- Create and affirm VALUES & PRACTICES that resist abuse and oppression and encourage safety, support, and accountability.
- Develop sustainable strategies to ADDRESS COMMUNITY MEMBERS' ABUSIVE BEHAVIOR, and create a process for them to account for their actions and transform their behavior.
- Commit to the ongoing development of all members of the community, and of the community itself, in order to TRANSFORM THE POLITICAL CONDITIONS that reinforce oppression and violence.
- Provide SAFETY & SUPPORT to community members who are violently targeted that RESPECTS THEIR SELF-DETERMINATION.[8]

I think what's important about INCITE!'s approach is that community is more than just a group of individuals; it can be a set of common values or affiliations that provide the connection necessary to hold someone accountable. Communities must be built up proactively so they have the courage to hold their members accountable when necessary. Another strength is INCITE!'s understanding that the criminal justice system is inherently flawed and does nothing to stop violence against women, especially women of color. To

---

8   Ibid., 291.

quote from their website, "In the end, the only thing that will stop violence against women of color is when our communities no longer tolerate it. Developing these strategies are difficult because they entail addressing the root causes of oppression—racism, sexism, homophobia, and economic exploitation—but in the end, it is only through building communities of resistance and accountability that we can hope to stop violence against women of color."[9]

To me, safer spaces are sanctuaries—places of refuge and safety. A safe space is like the protection I wish my uncle had when he was murdered in 2016 in my childhood neighborhood of West Baltimore while sitting on the steps of a friend's house to relax after a long hard day at work. Not having access to safe spaces also affects men, which is why we need to prioritize creating more of them.

I need safer spaces because they help me escape from the chaos of the world. Safer spaces provides me with opportunities to let go and be my authentic self without the constraints of modern society. They teach me to unlearn and question everything I have ever been taught about my worth in spaces as a Black woman in a racist, sexist society. They have empowered me to always step up and fight back against anything

---

9   INCITE! Women of Color Against Violence, "Community Accountability Working Document," INCITE!, https://incite-national .org/community-accountability-working-document.

that is actively working to erase my rights and entire existence.

The most important thing people can do to provide a safe space is by being as diverse and flexible as possible because it looks different for everyone. What is safe for me is not the same type of safety for everyone else, however, if given the tools and resources to create these spaces, we can make the world a better place.

—Brittany Oliver,
founder Not Without Black Women

Communities Against Rape and Abuse

CARA was an organization in Seattle that advocated "a broad agenda for liberation and social justice while prioritizing antirape work as the center of our organizing." They used "community organizing, critical dialogue, artistic expression, and collective action as tools to build safe, peaceful, and sustainable communities." Although CARA no longer exists, the INCITE! website describes an instructive example of how they approached accountability, developing a model that worked for them while trying to get an organization to hold a perpetrator accountable. "First, the survivor worked with a supportive organization to develop strategies to address the situation. Then, she developed a collective of allies within the organization, including male allies. These male allies confronted the perpetrator with the demand that he resign his positions of power, leave the organization, and seek counseling. These allies then follow[ed] his progress. The idea was not so much ostracism, but for him to not be in positions of power within progressive groups."[10]

Did you catch all the key elements? The plan for dealing with the situation was victim-led. She had a support group and a separate but connected group of allies in charge of confronting the person accused of harm. They had a clearly laid-out list of actionable requests, and the male allies were entrusted to hold him accountable by keeping track of his progress, presumably until he could hold himself accountable and be let back into the fold again. This way the victim never had to have contact with her abuser if she didn't want to. While the account doesn't give any details about what happened after this specific process, it's unlikely that man would ever hold a position of real power in their group again, but he was not shunned or made to feel disposable.

Creative Interventions

Like most of the projects mentioned in this chapter, Creative Interventions was started in response to the lack of options given to victims and community members who wanted to end interpersonal violence. Focusing mainly on domestic violence and sexual assault, they worked with partner organizations in the San Francisco Bay Area and spent three years developing an alternative strategy for dealing with harm. One of their main goals is to "shift the anti-violence movement away from individualized social services and criminalization towards community-based responses to violence."[11] The

10 Ibid.

11 "CI Goals and Objectives," Creative Interventions, http://www.creative-interventions.org/about/ci-goals-objectives.

uniqueness of their approach can be seen in the list of questions their project seeks to answer:

- How can family members, friends, neighbors, coworkers and community members get actively involved in ending violence when their own loved ones are experiencing interpersonal violence? These people are what we end up calling community allies or what others might call bystanders or social network.
- How can we use our connection and care for people who are victims or survivors of violence to not only provide safety but also opportunities for them to heal and reconnect to healthier relationships?
- How can we all provide greater safety for survivors or victims of violence even if they stay with or need to co-exist in the same community with people who have harmed them?
- How can we get violent or abusive people to stop the harm they have caused, repair it—and change their attitudes and behavior so that they become part of the solution?
- How can we change violent behavior by using our connection and care for people who have caused harm rather than by using threats, punishment or policing?
- How can we change everyday beliefs, practices and skills to address, reduce, end and prevent violence?
- How can we use all of the above to create the safe, respectful and healthy communities that we all seek?[12]

---

12   Preface to *Creative Interventions Toolkit: A Practical Guide to Stop Interpersonal Violence* (Creative Interventions, 2018), http://www

From that starting point, they created their own easy-to-follow toolkit, based on actual interventions and research. It's free and readily available online—all 608 pages. All of their experience in conducting community-based interventions is laid out, step by step, in a visually appealing PDF. If your town has no restorative or transformative justice organizations or options, I highly recommend using the Creative Interventions' guide as a starting place to facilitate your own community-based solutions.

Chrysalis Collective

The Chrysalis Collective began in response to a specific incident of acquaintance rape within their activist circle. Taking their cues from the victim, a group of "womyn and trans folk of color" came up with a plan to hold the accused accountable for their actions, without involving the police or justice system. Throughout the process, they were mindful of the power imbalances between the victim and the "aggressor" (their preferred term for someone who has harmed), as well as the potential for everyone in their community to grow and learn from the experience.

Based on that initial incident, they wrote a very helpful guide about their process, describing their thoughts and concerns, how they planned for everyone's safety, and their overall goals every step of the way, from when they were first told about the rape all the way to accountability meetings with the aggressor. They broke their process down to a number of clear and discrete steps that have been helpful to many groups seeking to develop their own transformative accountability

.creative-interventions.org/tools/toolkit.

processes. I'll give a brief overview but highly recommend going to the source.[13]

1. Gathering: form a survivor support team (SST). This involves asking the sorts of questions listed in the INCITE! section above but also assessing the capacities and availability of team members as well as figuring out what resources they will need.

2. Expanding: form an accountability team. This is the team that works with the aggressor to hold him accountable. The teams are separate so that members of the SST can focus on the victim's healing and because many of them may not feel capable of working compassionately with the abuser. This should start with coming up with a list of ideal attributes for team members who will remain committed to a "survivor-centered praxis."

3. Communicating: define the relationship between teams. As the teams have different but related goals, it's important to be clear about expectations and roles, as well as what will need to be communicated (such as the abuser's progress and the victim's needs) and how.

4. Storming and developing: create a transformative justice plan. This, like everything else thus far, is done before the abuser is approached, so that everyone is clear what the steps toward transformative justice are,

---

13 Chrysalis Collective, "Beautiful, Difficult, Powerful: Ending Sexual Assault Through Transformative Justice," in Ching-In Chen, Jai Dulani, and Piepzna-Samarasinha, eds., *Revolution Starts at Home*.

how to guide the abuser forward, and what sorts of problems might arise.

5. Summoning: prepare for the first approach. This involves gathering all the resources you'll need: local transformative justice services, lists of therapists and men's groups, et cetera. It's also when you decide the how of the approach: who will do the talking, where it will all go down, et cetera.

6. Building: the first meeting with the aggressor.

7. Transforming: ongoing meetings with the accountability team. If things go well, then the aggressor has agreed to participate in an accountability process, which will be mean ongoing work, meetings, and assessments of progress. This is theoretically where his "transformation" begins.

8. Evaluating: lessons learned.

Again, read the Chrysalis account. It's a very helpful and clear plan to draw from. I especially appreciate the way they describe all the issues that came up during the process that they did not anticipate, like having to balance the victim's needs for privacy with the desire to keep the community at large informed of the aggressor's behavior, or how easy it was to forget to check in on the victim while they concentrated on the aggressor's journey. The broadest lessons to learn from their experience would be to always center the victim, do your research, come up with a plan, follow through, and be patient and intentional.

Forgiveness Circle

We're trying to think of new ways to conceive of justice, right? Well, let's get extreme.

There is an interesting story about an African tribe's approach to wrongdoing that has been circulating for years. It is all over the internet and has shown up in a number of books including Leonard Zunin's self-help book *Contact: The First Four Minutes* and Alice Walker's *We Are the Ones We Have Been Waiting For*. Here's the version that appears in the latter:

> In the Babemba tribe of South Africa, when a person acts irresponsibly or unjustly, he is placed in the center of the village, alone and unfettered.
>
> All work ceases, and every man, woman, and child in the village gathers in a large circle around the accused individual. Then each person in the tribe speaks to the accused, one at a time, each recalling the good things the person in the center of the circle has done in his lifetime. Every incident, every experience that can be recalled with any detail and accuracy, is recounted. All his positive attributes, good deeds, strengths, and kindnesses are recited carefully and at length.
>
> This tribal ceremony often lasts for several days. At the end, the tribal circle is broken, a joyous celebration takes place, and the person

is symbolically and literally welcomed back
into the tribe.[14]

Now that you've read it, let me be clear: this story may
not be true. Its origins are unknown, and no version I've seen
cites a reliable source.

That doesn't matter for our purposes. The point is: as you
read it, could you imagine it? Did it seem unrealistic? Wrong?
Did it make you uncomfortable? Hopeful? Well, we have to
be willing to start thinking in such "extreme" ways if we want
to break away from our current punitive logic. The solution,
as they say, looks nothing like the problem. There are various
forms of forgiveness and accountability circles being used in
the real world. Maybe this idea seems like too much to you;
maybe it's not right for your situation; maybe you aren't ready
for that level of forgiveness. That's fine. Take it just as an option to keep in mind.

And also keep this in mind: on one of the internet sites
that published the story above, the widow of Leonard Zunin
left an interesting comment about what she thought the
story meant to him: "This wondrous process isn't about forgiveness as much as it is about reminding the community
and especially the person who has transgressed that they are
beautiful and worthy. By sharing tales of their good deeds
and good qualities, the transgression is seen as part of the
whole of the person's life. We will all misstep, no matter how
hard we try to live a just life. So the ceremony ends with

---

14 Alice Walker, *We Are the Ones We Have Been Waiting For: Inner Light in
a Time of Darkness*, (New York: New Press, 2006), 203.

celebration and re-commitment to seeing the good in others and in ourselves."[15]

Preventing Harm: The Talking Circle

In addition to responding appropriately to specific harm done, proactively building a strong community can interrupt cycles of harm as or before they happen. When #MeToo broke, I led a discussion for local men who were interested in what actions they could take to become better male allies. From that discussion, we decided to create a men's group, essentially a talking circle, where men and people benefiting from male privilege could get together and talk about common hurdles they face when trying to implement feminist practices into their lives. A talking circle like this is great for a group of similar people (common age, gender, or recurring issues) to 1) meet on a regular basis, 2) give voice to their feelings and concerns, 3) sort through their experiences and learn how to support each other, problem-solve together, and find ways to be a positive part of their community. Meeting monthly, our male ally group will read and discuss certain articles or books, invite local nonprofits to share their perspective on pressing local issues for women and LGBTQIA folks, and practice tough conversations. By learning from each other and challenging their own biases, this group is able to be better feminists, making it easier to challenge any sexist behavior exhibited by their friends and family. After all, if you are used to meeting up and expressing yourself in healthy, constructive

---

15 Hilary Zunin, comment on "How Babemba Tribe Forgives," KindSpring, September 26, 2007, https://www.kindspring.org/story/view.php?sid=7535.

ways when things are good or low stress, then it will be easier to do so when things are more complicated.

Build and Sustain

Building safer spaces and maintaining them takes work. People are complex and spaces are unique. Addressing harm has no one-size-fits-all approach. I asked Melanie Keller, co-creator of the Safer Spaces Program of Baltimore and my dear friend, to write something for this book. Her reflections on the trainings we ran in the early days capture the complexities and necessity of doing this work, as well as the necessity of talking honestly about harassment. So I'm going to quote her at length:

> The most important, and my favorite, part of the Hollaback! Baltimore Safer Spaces campaign was always the group discussion part of the mandatory training sessions. We first discuss what the Safer Spaces campaign is, why it's important and what signing onto it means for everyone present. Then the group discussion begins once we open the floor to the trainees and ask about the kinds of situations or complaints that they usually encounter. Every type of space has its own issues based on its physical layout, purpose, the collective's organizational structure, etc.; the response to harassment has to adjust accordingly. This group discussion was almost always the first time that any space had come

together to talk openly and only about harassment. Considering how rampant harassment in bars really is, it is mind-boggling to think that employees in any bar in Baltimore City had full staff meetings before, but harassment was never a topic or never the purpose of the meeting.

Providing this opportunity for everyone to sit together and only talk about harassment with expert facilitators was an integral part of the campaign, and to me it was completely nonnegotiable. If you wanted to sign our pledge, the majority of your staff or members had to attend and participate in these trainings. They were always difficult to schedule, but we tried to be as flexible as possible and even did multiple training sessions for the same space to offer everyone several dates of trainings to choose from. In sticking so strongly to this requirement and believing in the transformative power of story-sharing, my hope was that this group discussion would be just the first of many for these spaces. I hoped that this would start a good habit after people recognized how necessary and useful these types of frank, difficult conversations were.

People would share stories of harassment happening in their space and discuss how frequent or rare specific instances were. They would detail how they handled things in the moment and whether they thought they could've done something better. Hollaback! Baltimore would facilitate a brainstorming session with the group to find alternative solutions. People would chime in with different ideas and we really worked through them to see how these solutions could likely impact the harassed, the space itself, all the people in it, and ultimately the external business or collective. This was a wonderful role-playing exercise that helped spaces work towards establishing norms for how the unique harassment incidents in their space were to be handled from then on. People also shared incidents that they felt they had responded to well and we would pick apart why it worked so well. Again, all of this was in an effort to create norms of response: when X happens, in this space we handle it by doing A usually, but sometimes B or C depending on the circumstances.

I learned so much from these group discussions about the complexities of coordinating a fun, safe, and comfortable social space. I learned new strategies from the trainees, who honestly were not all new to these ideas, and many times they knew much better than I how to handle things. It was helpful for all involved to work through tough scenarios of harassment together and address issues as a community. The group discussion and role play is where the facts and figures from the beginning of the training and the victim-based approach from the crisis response portion all come together and make sense. There were always more reluctant participants who seemed completely unimpressed by the whole campaign, but during the group discussion it was so encouraging to see these particular participants suddenly "get it" and add their own commentary once their coworker or colleague shared a story of harassment that they had never heard before.

While agreeing upon norms of response for each space when harassment occurs, it was clear that not everyone in the space had the same priorities and boundaries. A foundational part of this process was first negotiating what the space's collective priorities would be—obviously, safety from harassment for women and LGBTQ folks. Hollaback! Baltimore would at times have to reiterate facts and figures and re-make the case for prioritizing these marginalized groups. Then, once their priorities were clear, what those priorities look like in action exactly when harassment happened had to be crystal clear and role-playing exercises became easier to work through and standard responses surfaced with little effort.

As an aside, the power dynamics within these group discussions were unsurprisingly reflective of wider societal dynamics in general. Most of the first story-sharers were women and LGBTQ folks themselves. This was the perfect opportunity for any marginalized folks in a bar, restaurant, collective, etc. to share their experiences and simultaneously have organizational support from us and (finally) recognition from their fellow colleagues or members. Most of the people who responded, asked questions, and offered suggestions were definitely men, and usually White men. As a facilitator, I was acutely aware of this and worked to counteract it during each session. I would openly remind (or simply cut off) any one person who took up too much space and time to talk, usually White men, to please sit down and let others speak. In this way, we weren't just discussing, presenting, and theorizing healthy norms, but Hollaback! Baltimore was modeling exactly the facilitation behavior we would like to see others do in the future—watch how we handle this; you can definitely do it, too! (Melanie Keller, linguistics PhD candidate, cat mom, and former Hollaback! Baltimore co-director)

I am so grateful that you have read this book. It has been a bit of a one-sided conversation, I know, but the point really is for you to take it from here and start your own conversations in the spaces that are important to you. Like Mel says, they are invaluable.

Reading this book is as close to one of our trainings as I can give you. While nothing will beat sitting down in a group to discuss these topics and practicing the tactics with role-playing exercises (hint, hint; what are your plans later?), you can use this text as your reference point to begin building safer spaces wherever you go. So work this book—and do the work. Were there any bits that just didn't click, that you were hesitant to listen to? Congrats! Now you know where your weak points are and can address them. Do what you can, then figure out how you can do more. Keep a steady pace and take care of yourself, though. It's easy to burn out, but you, your ideas, and your energy are needed in the struggles ahead.

Luckily you don't have to do this work on your own. Share this book, or at least the basic ideas inside, with others and create your community in a way that is safe, welcoming, and fun for everyone.

APPENDIX

SAMPLE POSTERS
AND POSTCARDS

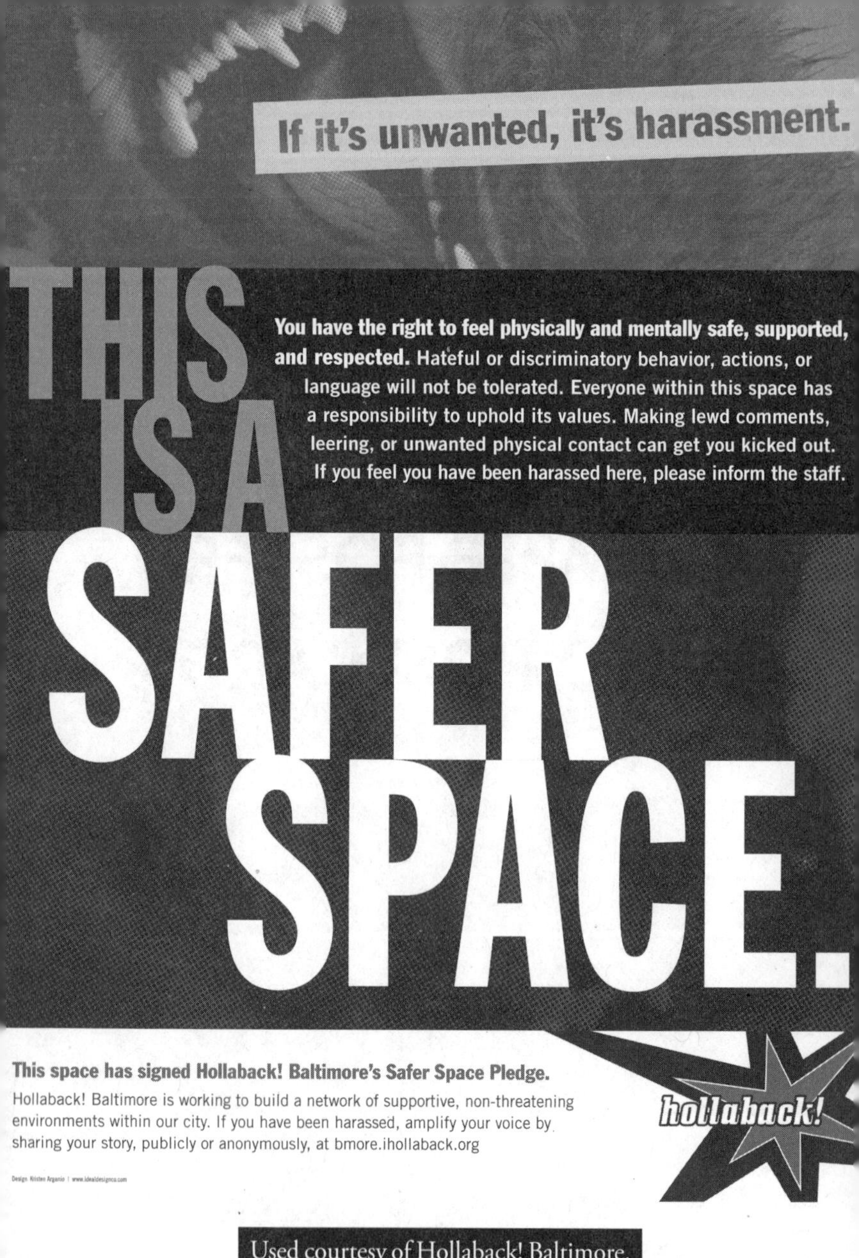

Used courtesy of Hollaback! Baltimore.

STAFF ADVICE FOR RESPONDING TO REPORTS OF HARASSMENT

Your place of work has signed up to the international Good Night Out Campaign, joining hundreds of licensed premises in a commitment to ending harassment on nights out. Whatever your job, you have a role to play!

BELIEVE THEM

This is rule number one, and the easiest way to support a person coming to you with an issue. They may feel embarassed or blame themselves. Posters help create an environment that doesn't tolerate harassment, but the way staff respond makes the biggest impact.

LISTEN

Letting a person speak is crucial. They may not want you to eject a harasser or 'make a fuss' for their own safety. REMEMBER: TWO SECOND RULE.

DON'T ASSUME

Use 'I..' sentences not 'you..' statements

Don't play judge and jury. Just stay calm and **pass up to your manager** as soon as you can.

People often minimise their own experiences. If you're hearing about an issue, it may well have happened to multiple people that night.

THE LAW

The law says that if a person touches someone else without their **consent,** and the touching is sexual, that's Sexual Assault and is a criminal offence!
(Sexual Offences Act 2003)

CONSENT means agreeing by choice, and having the freedom and 'capacity' to make that choice. This means that if someone is drunk or on drugs, they may not always be able to give consent.

REMEMBER TO LOG ALL REPORTS OF HARASSMENT IN YOUR INCIDENT BOOK DON'T HESITATE TO CALL 999 OR 101 IF NEEDED

See the list of participating venues and find out more at:
www.goodnightoutcampaign.org

ZERO TOLERANCE

hollaback!
BYSTANDER INTERVENTION

WHAT IS HARASSMENT?

Harassment is sexual, gender-based, and bias-motivated harassment and hate violence. At its core it is a power dynamic that constantly reminds historically marginalized groups of our vulnerability to assault in public spaces.

SEXUAL	GENDER-BASED	BIAS	HATE

HARASSMENT IN PUBLIC SPACE

CAN BE sexist, racist, religion-based, xenophobic, transphobic, homophobic, ableist, sizeist, classist

IS an expression of the interlocking and overlapping oppressions we face in public space and online

→ **HARASSMENT IS NEVER YOUR FAULT** ←

BADASS BYSTANDER MOVES: THE FIVE D'S

The Five D's are different methods you can use to support someone who's being harassed.

DIRECT	DISTRACT	DELEGATE	DOCUMENT	DELAY
Confront the situation. Be firm, clear, and concise.	Take an indirect approach to de-escalate the situation. *Ask for the time or directions	Seek help from a third party.	If it is safe to do so, document the incident.	Check in with the person being harassed.

DOCUMENTATION TIPS

KEEP A SAFE DISTANCE	FILM LANDMARKS	STATE THE DAY AND TIME

Always ask the person who was harassed what they want to do with the recording or screen shot. Never post it online or use it without their permission.

ONCE YOU'VE ACTED, SHARE YOUR STORY ON HOLLABACK!
YOU'LL INSPIRE OTHERS TO TAKE ACTION, AND GIVE HOPE TO PEOPLE WHO EXPERIENCE HARASSMENT ON THE REGULAR THAT THERE ARE FOLKS OUT THERE READY TO HAVE THEIR BACKS.

YOU HAVE THE POWER TO END HARASSMENT.

SKIMPY, TIGHT CLOTHING DOES NOT MEAN YES.

Consent is unmistakable.
If it isn't an enthusiastic yes, don't proceed.

DRINKING DOES NOT EQUAL CONSENT.

Consent is unmistakable.
If it isn't an enthusiastic yes, don't proceed.

These slogans (and approximately thirty others) were designed by Katy Hamm for Lesley University. Posters they appeared on also included contact info for numerous campus and off-campus support services. Used by permission of the artist.

APPENDIX

PUBLIC POLICIES

Short & Sweet

We are a safer space for LGBTQI folks, POC groups, punks,
lawyers, cyclists, trivia nerds, and almost everyone else.
The Pinhook, music venue, Durham, NC

We invite, welcome, and celebrate all
identities and expressions!
Safe Space Cafe, meetup group, Gainesville, FL

Theater X

*[Written by Laura Mateczun, these Audience Rights
and Responsibilities (posted on Theater X's website) are
a great way to let people know your values in advance
and that you care about all your patrons. The inclusion
of "responsibilities" lets audiences know that respect is a
two-way street. Just because someone is performing or
in costume does not mean they deserve harassment.]*

Audience Rights and Responsibilities

At Theater X, we believe audience members are artists as well. This list of rights and responsibilities for all visitors to Theater X attending plays, special events, or other programmatic activity, is non-exhaustive. It is intended as an outline of our principles and expectations as an organization. Theater X is an inclusive space at the nexus of experimental theater and community engagement. We work towards realizing the values of accessibility, equity, and dignity each day so that those who enter our space may create and enjoy the arts together. This specifically includes people of color, and people of all ages, abilities, gender expressions and identities, sexual orientations, education status, cultural backgrounds, and religious affiliations, or lack thereof.

The foundation of these values includes:

- Treating every person with dignity and respect;
- Being fair, considerate, and honest when interacting with all; and
- Rejecting violent or discriminatory behavior.

If you require immediate assistance, please speak to the nearest staff member.

Rights

- To feel safe
- To be treated with respect
- To have your comments and concerns heard
- To have your accessibility needs addressed, to the extent that we can
- To dress and express yourself comfortably and truly

Responsibilities

- Do not act or speak in a discriminatory manner, or use racist, sexist, transphobic, homophobic, or xenophobic language.
- Do not touch audience or cast members unless permission is expressly given in the production.
- Do not engage in any form of abuse, sexual misconduct, or violent behavior.
- Do not bring violent weapons into the space, such as loaded gun.
- Do not enter the backstage or prop storage space, unless given express permission by Theater X staff.
- Pay attention to important emergency evacuation and other safety procedures.
- Please return your program after the show if you are not going to keep it.
- Take your trash with you when you leave. (Please recycle!)

Isotope Comic Lounge

[The statement of this comic book store is posted on their website]

There was a time when I didn't think our little comic book shop needed to have a Harassment Policy. I was wrong. As a leader in the comics industry it's up to folks just like us to step up and let our industry know what behavior is socially acceptable, and what is not. Here at the Isotope it is our goal to create an environment where everyone is treated with dignity, courtesy and respect—and I know that people who regularly attend our events, shop at the store, or know any member of our Isotope family even a little can be confident that if they tell us someone is behaving poorly we will ask that ill-mannered person to leave. But what of those people who are at the Isotope for their first time? Our industry is going through some radical changes and the Isotope wants to be part of a positive change for the better. So we're putting this in writing.

The Isotope will not tolerate harassment of our guests of any kind. This includes unwanted, unwelcome or uninvited physical contact or attention, offensive verbal comments, inappropriate jokes or propositions, stalking, harassing photography or recording, or any other behavior which makes a person feel humiliated, intimidated or offended in regards, but not limited, to their race, age, gender, gender identity, sexual orientation, religion, disability, appearance, body type, color, creed, origin or simply who they are.

People who violate this policy will be given an official First Warning by either a member of our staff or any member of our community. This warning may be phrased in an official sounding capacity such as "that is a violation of Isotope's Harassment Policy" or it may be phrased in a more casual manner such as, but not limited to, "that makes me uncomfortable" or "that is inappropriate" and even "hey not cool, man." These too are considered an official First Warning. There will be no Second Warning. If the behavior does not change, the offending party will simply be told they need to leave and be politely escorted out.

We realize that even the best of humans are flawed, imperfect beings, and with so many of our visitors coming from different parts of the world and walks of life, that some cultural differences may occur. And different people might have conflicting definitions of what "harassment" is. So everyone here is afforded the chance to correct a social faux pas. But you won't get two. Those who can't muster up the decency to respect each other, our community, the Isotope and also themselves just aren't welcome. Officially.

And because the Isotope is **your** community as well as ours, we deputize each and every one of you to take part in the enforcement of this policy. Which means that your Harassment Policy warning is just as official as mine is. In the event of an uncomfortable or awkward situation we still ask that all parties treat everyone at the Isotope with the kindness and respect they are due as fellow human beings. Even if they are jerks.

Our policy applies to all guests, including featured creators and also ourselves and staff. And even the music we play. Simply, if it's gotta go, then it's gotta go. This Harassment Policy is in effect at the Isotope always and forever. We will be adding a link to this post on every special event we announce so that this policy is clear to one and all.

Let's work together, like Zan and Jayna, to co-activate our Wonder Twin powers for a better world of comics! The Isotope has grown over the years as people and an entity, and we will continue to evolve for the betterment of ourselves, our community and the greater comics industry. So let's join forces… my fellow comic fans, fellow retailers and industry leaders… for a higher community standard and a greater, more welcoming comics industry for all.

Thank you to all of you for helping us build and better our amazing Isotope community.

Riot Fest

[The folks at this music festival worked with Our Music, My Body, to create a very clear anti-harassment policy that they posted on their website. Check out the whole thing to see the music-festival-specific examples. Below is a short sample.]

Riot Fest believes everyone should feel safe during the music festival. We will help maintain this by not tolerating harmful behaviors, which may include non-consensual touching or verbal harassment. If a participant chooses to break these policies they may be removed from the fest. If someone or something makes you feel uncomfortable or unsafe, no matter how minor it may seem, please do not stay silent. You can report it to any Riot Fest staff member and they will follow your lead and work with you to try to make sure it does not happen again and that you continue to feel safe at our festival.

Riot Fest has a **ZERO TOLERANCE POLICY** for harassment of any kind, including but not limited to: race, color, national origin, gender, gender identity, gender presentation, sexual orientation, age, body size, disability, appearance, religion, citizenship, pregnancy.

Harassment includes but is not limited to: stalking, verbal or physical intimidation, offensive verbal comments, physical assault and/or battery, harassing or non-consensual photography or recording, bathroom policing, inappropriate physical contact, unwelcome physical attention.

Suggested Tweets

If you're harassed at a show, just let our staff know! Everyone deserves to have a fun, harassment-free night. #makingspacessafer

Reminder: we do not allow harassment, bigotry, or violence of any kind at our venue! If u are harassed, tell staff immediately or message us here—we've got your back! #makingspacessafer

Suggested Blog Post

[This is a version of the suggested text provided to venues who have signed onto the Hollaback! Baltimore Safer Space Campaign. Feel free to pick and choose what works for you!]

We at [venue name] are excited to announce that we are working to become a safer space, based on the tactics outlined in *Making Spaces Safer* by Shawna Potter. We share her vision: a world where street harassment is not tolerated and where we all enjoy equal access to public spaces. [personal statement about why joining the campaign matters to you, or how you can specifically help those that are street harassed] After [reading *Making Spaces Safer*/attending a workshop by Shawna Potter/etc], our staff is ready for any situation; we are trained to remove anyone who is harassing women, people of color, or members of the LGBTQIA communities in our [space/venue/shop/etc.]. This includes leering, rude comments, touching, and any other behavior that makes you feel uncomfortable. Please notify our staff immediately of any issues you encounter. We will be happy deal to deal with the situation.

If you would like to report a problem anonymously, please contact us at [your email]. If you would like to learn more about Hollaback! Baltimore, the Safer Space Campaign, or actions you can take to help end street harassment, visit their website at: https://bmore.ihollaback.org/.

APPENDIX

INTERNAL DOCUMENTS

PUNK CLUB CONFLICT RESOLUTION PLAN

[A small DIY venue in Baltimore decided to draft a conflict resolution plan after realizing that, without one, they had no idea what to do when serious issues arose. It's simple yet thorough. The name of the venue has been changed for privacy]

Conflict Resolution Plan
A Means of Resolving Contentious Issues within a Community

Drafted and Approved by the Members of SOMETHING SOMETHING PUNK VENUE

The following document provides a conflict resolution plan for SOMETHING SOMETHING PUNK VENUE and consists of a step-by-step guide for dealing with an accusation of one of our members acting in a way conflicting with our mission statement, particularly instances of gender-based violence and racial discrimination.

1. Introduction and Reasoning Behind Conflict Resolution Plan
   a. Plan development and purpose:
      i. Arising from a series of conflicts between members and non-members in the summer of 2010, which had stemmed from an earlier conflict involving accusations of sexual assault, and the consequences emerging from it, in August 2011 members of SOMETHING SOMETHING PUNK VENUE (SSPV) moved to develop a conflict resolution plan to prevent a similar situation in the future.
      ii. The plan, which is laid out here, should be seen as a living document that can and should be continuously evaluated, as to ensure that a safe space (defined below) exists within SSPV for both members and non-members.
      iii. The plan is intended to hold members and non-members accountable to the Space's mission statement.
      iv. While the plan aims to respect individuals' confidentiality, certain issues that may be brought to SSPV may require members to refer individuals to outside mediation, counseling, or other professional services.
2. Definitions
   a. **Conflict**: A state of disharmony between incompatible or antithetical persons, ideas, or interests.
   b. **Conflict resolution plan**: A means of addressing conflict and attempting to resolve the issues contributing to its emergence; may involve dialogue, mediation, arbitration, etc.

c. **Safe space**: An environment in which everyone feels comfortable in expressing themselves and participating fully, without fear of attack, ridicule or denial of experience.

3. Plan of Action: Two Options

   a. The following steps would be taken upon receiving verbal or written notice of a member or individual attending an event at SSPV acting in a manner that contrasts with the Space's mission statement:

      i. Identification of conflict and those individuals affected by it

      ii. Ask that member to remove him/herself from SSPV activities until the conflict can be resolved. (This would not be a suspension or anything assuming guilt, but a temporary measure to help find resolution with some clarity.)

      iii. Within a period of two (2) weeks, a general meeting of all SSPV members must be called and be briefed on the situation at hand

      iv. At said meeting, members may volunteer to formulate a mediation team; ideally this group consists of at least three (3) individuals

      v. Upon confirmation of internal mediation group, independent meetings will be held with each party in order to collect information relevant to conflict and assess difficulty level

      vi. After conducting meetings with involved parties, mediation group will meet and discuss possible solutions to conflict

      vii. Proposed solutions will be offered to the general membership for review and approval

viii. After receiving approval from general membership, solutions will be presented to conflict participants

ix. If solutions are accepted, conflict resolution commitment is hereafter complete .

x. If solutions are rejected, outside mediation assistance will be determined

xi. Internal mediation group will contact a mediation group that has nothing to do with either party or SSPV (a list of such groups should be created ahead of time) and explain the situation

xii. The decision of either mediator group stands and is final.

b. In instances involving the need for more privacy and care for more sensitive and traumatic incidents, including, but not limited to gender-based violence, racial discrimination:

i. The one who brings forth a complaint may decide how to be referred to (victim, survivor, accuser, party A, etc.) and the collective must respect that. They may also choose to instead go through the original SSPV CRP mediation process, but they cannot be made to feel pressured to do so

ii. Each party will obtain their own advocate who would then present their side to an objective mediator

iii. After presenting a list of potential three advocates, each party must obtain the other party's approval for their own advocate and reserves the right to reject the proposed advocate selection

iv. Should either party feel uncomfortable with an advocate the accused or victim recommended, they would be able to present their reasons for rejection—perhaps a conflict of interest, something along those lines—and the particular advocate will not be present

v. The objective mediator is to be agreed upon by the SSPV collective members without the individual parties being present

vi. Prior to proceeding, the parties will immediately come to a safe space agreement, which may include the following feature: Determination of what individuals may attend SSPV shows or other events while the mediation process takes place

vii. For the purpose of privacy and confidentiality, the victim will decide what is acceptable for their advocate to present to the mediator

viii. The mediation team is to keep the SSPV collective updated on general status (ex: "It's still going on," "last meeting coming up," etc.), but all that is discussed or decided will remain private between the team until being informed of the final outcome, if necessary. The decision of the mediation team is to be final.

ix. If the accused party refuses to participate in the mediation they will forfeit their right to remain a collective member

4. List of Possible Mediators in the Local Area [this is a great spot to list any local resources that would help your group through conflict—counselors, mediators, and alternative justice organizations, for example]

THEATER X
CODE OF CONDUCT

[Groups need public and private policies in place to help prevent discrimination and violence, but if you are going to have policies you also need predetermined procedures for dealing with incidents when they inevitably occur. This document, written by Laura Mateczun, spells out basic anti-discrimination policies, grounding techniques, how to handle reports of harassment from audience members, and reporting protocol for volunteers/staff for internal issues.]

Code of Conduct

This code of conduct is intended to describe the expectations and responsibilities of volunteers, students, teachers, event and space renters, performers, tenants, company members, and board members of Theater X. As a radical organization, we aim to be an accessible, equitable, safe, and respectful space for all who wish to create and enjoy experimental theater. This specifically includes people of color, and people of all ages, abilities, gender expressions and identities, sexual orientations, education statuses, cultural backgrounds, and religious affiliations, or lack thereof. We believe all people have the right to dress and express themselves in the fashion most true to their identity.

The foundation of these expectations includes:

- Treating every person with dignity and respect;
- Being fair, considerate, and honest when interacting with all;
- Conducting oneself professionally; and
- Rejecting violent and discriminatory behavior.

Theater X will not tolerate discrimination, sexual harassment, or verbal, written, or physical abuse on its premises, or in any form.

1. **The following are expressly prohibited by Theater X:**
   a. Discrimination or bias-related harassment, based on actual or perceived age, ability, race, gender expression or identity, immigration status, sexual orientation, religious beliefs and practices, education status, accent, or nationality;
   b. All forms of harassment, including:
      i. verbal;
      ii. physical;
      iii. visual; or
      iv. written.
   c. Sexual misconduct, including, but not limited to:
      i. Creating a hostile environment;

      1. e.g., boasting or bragging about sexual activity; non-consensual lewd communications; or spreading of sexual rumors.

  ii. Quid pro quo ("this for that") transactional sexual harassment;

      1. e.g., threatening punishment; or offering reward.

  iii. Behavior which lacks consent, generally;

      1. i.e., does not have knowing, voluntary, and clear permission to engage in mutually agreed upon sexual activity, or goes beyond the boundaries of previously established consent.

  iv. Sexual misconduct, as defined by Maryland law;

  v. Sexual harassment;

  vi. Non-consensual sexual intercourse;

  vii. Non-consensual sexual contact;

  viii. Sexual exploitation;

      1. (e.g., sexual voyeurism; recording or photography of sexual activity, or dissemination thereof, without consent; engaging in sexual activity while knowingly infected with STI and without informing the other person; or administering alcohol or drugs to another person without their knowledge or consent.)

  ix. Intimate partner or relationship violence; and

  x. Stalking.

  d. Suggested, threatened, or actual violence toward any individual or protected group;

  e. Conduct endangering the life, safety, health, or well-being of others; and

f. Wanton and deliberate destruction of Theater X property, or another community member's personal property.

2. **Emergency Situations / Crisis Protocol**:
   a. In situations requiring an immediate response, please ensure these steps are taken:
      i. De-escalate the situation to the best of your ability (i.e., speak in calm tones with compassionate language, and utilize emotional grounding techniques)
         1. If this is not possible, take reasonable steps to remove the violating party from the situation, or premises.
      ii. Actively listen to what is being conveyed
      iii. Ask the aggrieved party what they would prefer you do:
         1. Keep an eye out and ensure a distinct separation of space;
         2. Talk to the individual and try and sort out the situation; or
         3. Remove the individual from the space.
   b. If necessary, Theater X may choose to utilize further conflict resolution procedures, as described below.

3. **Reportees**:
   a. Overall:
      i. Managing Director [name and email address]
      ii. Artistic Director [name and email address]
   b. Productions:
      i. Director of that production
      ii. Stage Manager of that production
   c. Designated Board Members:

     i. (TBD)

     ii. (TBD)

  d. Designated Company Member:

     i. (TBD)

  e. Tenant Relations:

     i. (TBD, tenant volunteer)

  f. Rental Relations:

     i. (TBD)

4. **Notice Is Required of Concurrently Developing Intimate Relationships**:

  a. i.e., those in which a direct supervisory power imbalance exists, such as teacher/student, or director/performer relationships.

  b. Such relationships should be promptly reported to the Artistic and Managing Directors, or the two designated board member Reportees, of Theater X.

     i. While all involved individuals may provide notice, the onus is on the individual with supervisory power to report the relationship.

     ii. The Reportees must then confirm the consensual nature of the relationship with the other individual involved.

5. **Reporting Protocol**:

  a. Report:

     i. "Reporter" is the person submitting the report.

       1. Any individual (i.e., member of the public) may be a Reporter.

       2. Access to this route of recourse does not require being a signatory to this code.

       3. The Reporter may choose to submit the report verbally, or in writing.

ii. "Reportee" is the person receiving the report.

 1. In order to ease any burden on the Reporter, the Reportee has the responsibility to compile all information relevant in the original report and later investigations, as described below.

iii. Those who experience, or witness, violations to this code should report the violation to any listed Reportee as promptly as possible.

iv. This report (either verbal or written) should include descriptions of:

 1. The situation;
 2. The wrongful behavior;
 3. The impact or effect it had on you;
 4. How you want the behavior of the accused to change;
 5. What you believe to be appropriate consequences if the behavior does not change; and
    a. Theater X recognizes that this may evolve over time.
    b. If so, reasonable measures should be taken to inform the relevant Reportees.
 6. If you prefer to follow an informal (§5b), or formal (§5c), conflict resolution procedure.

v. The Reportee must then forward a written description of the report to other relevant Reportees, depending on the expressed preferred resolution procedure, as described below.

 1. One Reportee must be someone with organizational authority, and come from the "Overall" Reportee category.

2. Best efforts should be made for relevant Reportees to be:
   a. From differing Reportee categories; and
   b. Removed from the immediate situation.
3. The Reporter's input will carry much weight as to who the desired relevant Reportees should be.
4. If necessary, this team will include an independent third party with subject matter expertise.

vi. If necessary, upon receipt of the report, Theater X may immediately implement remedial and responsive, or protective, actions including, but not limited to:
   1. No contact orders;
   2. Interim suspension upon investigation;
   3. Scheduling or role assignment accommodations;
   4. Limitations of access to the Theater X facility and other spaces managed by Theater X, for programming, rehearsals, or other public/special events; or
   5. Contract cancellation.

b. Informal Resolution:
   i. Involving informal discussion, or mediation, in a neutral environment, with at least two Reportees present.
   ii. Upon successful completion of the informal mediation session, in which the complaint is satisfied, or wrongful behavior is addressed, the attending Reportees will inform the parties involved, as well as the Theater X Board and management, in

writing, of completion, and provide any further recommendations.

   iii. The attending Reportees will recommend to the Theater X Board and management, in writing, that the formal resolution procedure (§5c) should be followed, if:

     1. the attempted informal mediation fails;

     2. the complaint is not satisfied; or

     3. the Reportees do not come to a unanimous decision.

c. Formal Resolution:

   i. The Theater X Board of Review, consisting of at least three Reportees not within the same reporting category, will investigate and review testimony, received in private interviews, as to the wrongful behavior.

   ii. If necessary, a third-party mediator may be enlisted.

   iii. The Board of Review will submit a written report to all involved parties, as well as the Theater X Board and management, as to its findings and unanimously recommended outcome.

d. The Reportees involved in the investigation have the authority to charge Theater X management with implementing the unanimously recommended outcome.

   i. If the accused party is the Artistic or Managing Director, board approval is required for implementation of the recommended outcome.

e. Retaliation or intimidation directed at any person who reports the occurrence of harassment or discrimination is not acceptable and will be considered a breach of this code.

f. The confidentiality and privacy of those involved will be respected throughout the investigation and conflict resolution process. Any relevant documents created in the duration of an informal or formal conflict resolution procedure will be destroyed, after a three-year retention period upon final resolution, depending on the severity of the outcome.

g. Anyone who is determined, after a reasonably speedy investigation, to have engaged in harassment or discrimination, or otherwise wrongful behavior in violation of these policies, or fails to cooperate with investigations, will see the consequence of up to complete severance of all relationships with Theater X, depending on the facts.

6. **Severability**: If any part of this code is declared unenforceable or invalid, the remainder will continue to be valid and enforceable.

7. **Conclusion**: Theater X establishes this code of conduct to hold ourselves to high standards of communication, collaboration, and artistry. It is meant to detail the principles we wish to model and exemplify in our everyday practice. However, we recognize this code unfortunately cannot contain answers and procedures for all situations that may arise, and the various complex and nuanced matters involved. The provisions included within this code will be carried out to the extent that is allowed under the law. This document is intended to be reviewed, critiqued,

and amended periodically to reflect the evolving nature of the Baltimore arts and experimental theater community.

_____

Name / Organization

_____

Signature

_____

Date

APPENDIX

RESOURCES

Book Recommendations

Adichie, Chimamanda Ngozi. *We Should All Be Feminists*. London: Fourth Estate, 2017.

Bongiovanni, Archie and Tristan Jimerson. *A Quick and Easy Guide to They/Them Pronouns*. Portland, OR: Limerence Press, 2018.

Chen, Ching-In, Jai Dulani, and Leah Lakshmi Piepzna-Samarasinha. *The Revolution Starts at Home: Confronting Intimate Violence within Activist Communities*. Chico, CA: AK Press, 2016.

Crabb, Cindy. *Learning Good Consent: On Healthy Relationships and Survivor Support*. Chico, CA: AK Press, 2016.

Dawes, Laina. *What Are You Doing Here? A Black Woman's Life and Liberation in Heavy Metal*. New York: Bazillion Points, 2012.

INCITE! *Color of Violence: The INCITE! Anthology*. Durham: Duke University Press, 2016.

hooks, bell. *Feminism Is for Everybody: Passionate Politics. 2nd ed.* London: Routledge, 2014.

Levine, Amir, and Rachel Heller. *Attached: The New Science of Adult Attachment and How It Can Help You Find—and Keep—Love*. New York: Jeremy P. Tarcher/Penguin, 2011.

Patterson, Jennifer, and Reina Gossett. *Queering Sexual Violence: Radical Voices from within the Anti-violence Movement.* Riverdale, NY: Riverdale Avenue Books, 2016.

Real, Terrence. *The New Rules of Marriage: What You Need to Know to Make Love Work.* New York: Ballantine Books, 2008.

Ritchie, Andrea J. *Invisible No More: Police Violence against Black Women and Women of Color.* Boston: Beacon Press, 2017.

Ryan, Christopher, and Cacilda Jethá. *Sex at Dawn: The Prehistoric Origins of Modern Sexuality.* Carlton North, Vic. (Australia): Scribe Publications, 2011.

Stryker, Kitty. *Ask: Building Consent Culture.* Portland, OR: Thorntree Press, 2017.

Urb, Claire. *It's Down to This: Reflections, Stories, Experiences, Critiques, and Ideas on Community and Collective Response to Sexual Violence, Abuse, and Accountability.* n.a.: It's Down to This, 2011.

What about the Rapists? Anarchist Approaches to Crime & Justice. Leeds (UK): Dysophia, 2015.

Zeisler, Andi. *We Were Feminists Once: From Riot Grrrl to CoverGirl®, the Buying and Selling of a Political Movement.* New York: Public Affairs, 2017.

Organizations

Hollaback! is a global, people-powered movement to end harassment. They work to understand the problem, ignite public conversations, and develop innovative strategies that ensure equal access to public spaces. They leverage the very spaces where harassment happens—from online to the streets—to have each other's backs, create communities of resistance, and build a world where we can all be who we are, wherever we are. Visit https://www.ihollaback.org/

Green Dot is providing schools and communities with programs and prevention strategies that address sexual assault, dating/domestic violence, bullying, and stalking. Visit https://alteristic.org/services/green-dot/

Circle of 6 is fast, easy-to-use, and private. The app, originally designed for college students to prevent sexual violence, is also handy for teenagers, parents, friends, and all communities seeking to foster healthy relationships and safety. It's the mobile way to look out for each other on campus or when you're out for the night. A simple tool to prevent violence before it happens. Visit: https://www.circleof6app.com/

INCITE! is a network of radical feminists of color organizing to end state violence and violence in our homes and communities. They provide a large list of resources online for self-education and organizing, as well as strategies for community accountability. Visit: https://incite-national.org/

Stop Street Harassment (SSH) is a one-stop shop. Founder Holly Kearl has written several books and conducted thorough research studies on the subject of street harassment. SSH also founded International Anti-Street Harassment Week and a national street harassment hotline with help of RAINN (Rape, Abuse and Incest National Network). Share your story, educate yourself, or get involved at http://www.stopstreetharassment.org/.

Online Transformative Justice Resources

Anti-Oppression Resource and Training Alliance (AORTA): http://aorta.coop/portfolio_page/supporting-survivors-of-sexual-assault/

Bay Area Transformative Justice Collective: https://batjc.wordpress.com/resources/

Centre for Justice and Reconciliation: http://restorativejustice.org/

Chrysalis Collective, "Beautiful, Difficult, Powerful: Ending Sexual Assault through Transformative Justice": http://www.blackandpink.org/wp-content/upLoads/Beautiful-Difficult-Powerful.pdf

Creative Interventions Toolkit: A Practical Guide to Stop Interpersonal Violence: http://www.creative-interventions.org/tools/toolkit/

Critical Resistance (Resources for Addressing Harm, Accountability, and Healing): http://criticalresistance.org/resources/addressing-harm-accountability-and-healing/

National Hotlines

General Crisis Counseling: Crisis Text Line provides free, 24/7 support for those in crisis. Text 741741 from anywhere in the United States to text with a trained crisis counselor. Every texter is connected with a crisis counselor, a real human being trained to bring texters from a hot moment to a cool calm through active listening and collaborative problem solving. Text SUPPORT to 741741 or visit http://www.crisistextline.org/.

Trans Lifeline: Trans Lifeline is a 501(c)3 nonprofit dedicated to the well-being of transgender people. They run a hotline staffed by transgender people for transgender people. Trans Lifeline volunteers are ready to respond to whatever support needs members of the trans community might have. Call (877) 565-8860 or, in Canada: (877) 330-6366, or visit https://www.translifeline.org/.

HIPS: HIPS promotes the health, rights, and dignity of individuals and communities impacted by sexual exchange and/or drug use due to choice, coercion, or circumstance. HIPS provides compassionate harm reduction services, advocacy, and community engagement that is respectful, nonjudgmental, and affirms and honors individual power and agency. HIPS offers a 24/7 hotline to provide emotional support, schedule supplies deliveries, and get connected to health and supportive services. Call (800) 676-4477.

National Street Harassment Hotline: In partnership with Defend Yourself and the Rape, Abuse and Incest National

Network (RAINN), Stop Street Harassment launched a gen-der-based street harassment national hotline. Help is available 24/7 in English and Spanish. Call 855-897-5910.

Rape, Abuse and Incest National Network (RAINN): RAINN is the nation's largest anti–sexual violence organization. In addition to the National Sexual Assault Hotline, RAINN also carries out programs to prevent sexual violence, help survivors, and ensure that perpetrators are brought to justice. Call 1-800-656-4673 or visit hotline.rainn.org/online to chat online with a RAINN Support Specialist.

Depression and Suicide

The Trevor Project: Crisis intervention and suicide prevention for LGBTQ youth. Their trained counselors are there to support you 24/7. If you are a young person in crisis, feeling suicidal, or in need of a safe and judgment-free place to talk, call the TrevorLifeline at 866-488-7386 or visit https://www.thetrevorproject.org/.

National Suicide Prevention Lifeline: The Lifeline provides 24/7, free and confidential support for people in distress, prevention and crisis resources for you or your loved ones, and best practices for professionals. Call (800) 273-8255 or visit https://suicidepreventionlifeline.org/.

Dating Abuse and Domestic Violence

Black Women's Blueprint: BWB specializes in helping traumatized women, cis and trans and LGBTQ survivors of crime, and abuse with counseling, support groups and sister circles. They serve youth and adults and their families, who have experienced one or more of the following: childhood sexual abuse or physical abuse, rape or sexual assault, human trafficking, physical assault. Call the Counseling Center: 347-533-9102 or 347-533-9103. Their Healing and Counseling Program coordinator will guide you on the phone through the steps to an appointment with a trauma healing expert. Their staff will help you assess your current needs, create a workable timetable and plan for your emotional recovery and healing, and find other services if and when necessary.

loveisrespect: loveisrespect's purpose is to engage, educate, and empower young people to prevent and end abusive relationships. Highly trained advocates offer support, information, and advocacy to young people who have questions or concerns about their dating relationships. They also provide information and support to concerned friends and family members, teachers, counselors, service providers, and members of law enforcement. Free and confidential phone, live chat, and texting services are available 24/7/365. Call 1-866-331-9474, visit loveisrespect.org to chat online, or text loveis to 22522.

National Domestic Violence Hotline: Their highly trained advocates are available 24/7/365 to talk confidentially with anyone experiencing domestic violence, seeking resources or information, or questioning unhealthy aspects of their relationship. Call 1-800-799-7233 or visit http://www.thehotline.org to chat online.

Child Abuse

Childhelp National Child Abuse Hotline: Serving the United States and Canada, the hotline is staffed 24/7 with professional crisis counselors who—through interpreters—provide assistance in over 170 languages. The hotline offers crisis intervention, information, and referrals to thousands of emergency, social service, and support resources. All calls are confidential. Call 1-800-422-4453.

National Safe Place: Safe Place provides access to immediate help and supportive resources for youth in need. As a community initiative, the program designates schools, fire stations, libraries, and other youth-friendly organizations as Safe Place locations, which display the yellow and black sign. Text SAFE and your current location 24/7 to 69866.

Runaways, Homeless, and At-Risk Youth

National Runaway Safeline: NRS is the go-to resource for America's runaway, homeless, and at-risk youth and their families, providing solution-focused support. Call 1-800-786-2929.

Miscellaneous

National AIDS Hotline: AIDS hotlines are invaluable for basic HIV/AIDS information. You can talk to someone knowledgeable about HIV and get referrals to various AIDS services in your city or state. The National AIDS hotline in Washington, D.C., is the only hotline open twenty-four hours a day, 365 days a year: 1-800-CDC-INFO.

This page has been intentionally left blank for you to fill in info about your local hotlines, resources, taxi numbers, and hospitals.

ACKNOWLEDGMENTS

I can't believe I was able to finish writing a pocket guide to safer spaces, let alone this entire book. This feat would not have been possible without the support of AK Press, the unending patience and expertise of my editor Charles Weigl, and the wisdom and experience of Melanie Keller and Corey Reidy, my fellow co-creators of the Safer Space Program. To Emily May and the entire Hollaback! community, your platform gave me a platform, and for that I will always be grateful. I'm so glad I found such a supportive network of badasses—when we amplify each other's voices, it becomes a roar that can't be ignored. To War On Women, band and crew, thank you for all our van discussions during boring drives; your perspectives make me a better feminist. (And thanks for letting me blather about safer spaces on the mic and hawk copies of the guide at the merch table.) To my friend Matt Morgan, any good work I have done over the last few years would not have been as good without your support. I could not have accomplished what I have without you. Thank you to Fusion Partnerships for handling all the boring yet necessary parts of running Hollaback! Baltimore, especially when I'm on the road. To everyone who contributed a personal story, I'm honored to have your voices included. To everyone who wanted to contribute but never got around to it, I know you're busy, and I still love you! To Sadie Dupuis for all the work you do and for getting my pocket guide into the hands of venues all around the country. To my critical readers this time around, Rahne Alexander, Melanie Keller, Lisa Root, Tyler Vile, and Sheila Wells, thank you for your perspectives, honesty, and speed. Thanks to everyone who's taken a workshop from me, hired me for feminist coaching, bought the pocket guide, and supported this effort in one way or another. Finally, my partner Brooks, for supporting this work in more ways than I can count. I'm done writing now, so we can start *The Office* from the top again.

ABOUT THE AUTHOR

At publication, Shawna Potter fronts the band War On Women, is ordained to perform wedding ceremonies, and is a repair tech and manager for Big Crunch Amp Repair and Design. The founder of Hollaback! Baltimore, she continues to speak publicly and train venues for their Safer Spaces Program and is available for speaking engagements, workshops, feminist coaching, and more. She's been interviewed on topics related to feminism, safer spaces, bystander intervention, and women in music in outlets like the *New York Times*, the *Washington Post*, *Noisey*, *Kerrang!*, *Alternative Press*, ThinkProgress, *PopSugar*, and *New Noise*. A constant TV watcher and compulsive straightener-upper, Shawna is not satisfied waiting for the world to change. She currently lives in Baltimore, Maryland, with her partner and a stack of books she'll get to one day. You can reach her at makingspacessafer@gmail.com to ask questions, book her for workshops and trainings, or to share stories of putting the tactics in this book into practice.